AF262978

PRAISE FROM THE ARENA

"Melissa has a long and successful record of being more than a leadership expert—she is a leadership innovator. She sees around corners, translates complexity into clarity, and gives leaders practical ways to perform under pressure. *Athleadership* is more than a book; it is a timely framework for how modern leaders must think and operate."

JAMAL MUASHSHER, President and CEO,
Valvoline Global Operations

"Melissa Dawn Simkins is the kind of advisor every executive needs in today's environment. Her strategic thinking and role as the pioneer of *Athleadership* bring rare systems-level clarity to the real complexity leaders face—connecting purpose, decision-making, culture, and performance through a proven operating model. I've witnessed Athleadership deliver measurable results, not just in how leaders think, but in how they lead, decide, and navigate change for themselves and their teams."

MONICA HAMMOND, Senior Vice President, Customer Success,
Verizon Consumer Group

"As a former student/professional athlete, and now an executive, life experience has shown me that lessons learned through playing sports go far beyond the game. Discipline, resilience, teamwork, and purpose shape leaders who can serve their families, businesses, and communities well. In her book, *Athleadership*, Melissa captures how the mindset developed in athletics prepares people to lead when it matters most."

TROY VINCENT, Executive Vice President, Football Operations,
National Football League (NFL)

"As an Olympic champion, I learned early that success under pressure is never accidental—it is the result of preparation, discipline, and mindset. In *Athleadership*, Melissa Dawn Simkins brilliantly connects the mental preparation elite athletes rely on with the realities leaders face every day. Her work captures a truth I've experienced both in sport and as a CEO: Performance when it matters most can be conditioned. This book offers a powerful framework for leaders who want to lead with resilience, clarity, and purpose when the stakes are highest."

BENITA FITZGERALD MOSLEY, OLY, CEO, US Center for SafeSport

"In *Athleadership*, Melissa Dawn Simkins explores the connection between elite athletic mindset, neuroscience, and the demands of leadership. Her reflections on preparation, accountability, resilience, and teamwork offer a thoughtful perspective for leaders seeking to strengthen performance and support their teams' growth."

JOHNNY C. TAYLOR JR., SHRM-SCP, President and CEO, SHRM

"Building a category taught me that leadership today isn't about playing it safe—it's about making decisions in uncertainty and driving impact that shapes industries. *Athleadership* feels less like another leadership program and more like a movement to build the kind of leaders this moment demands."

JULIE WAINWRIGHT, Author and Founder, The RealReal

"Melissa has been a key partner in helping our employees connect purpose to their leadership. She brings a visionary yet practical approach that strengthens clarity, resilience, and alignment. This work helped us translate insight into business impact by giving individuals the confidence they need to make decisions and lead when it matters most."

MICHELLE MURPHY, SVP and Chief Human Resources Officer,
BAE Systems, Inc.

"*Athleadership* isn't theory; it is proven to build the mindset, discipline, and resilience leaders need to perform at the highest level, no matter the arena."

"As someone working at the center of system-level change in college athletics, I have seen how much leadership must evolve to meet the moment. Melissa's work influenced me personally as much as professionally. She challenged how I think, decide, and show up in moments of pressure and transition. That perspective has shaped my own leadership journey and growth. It is about building leaders and organizations that are ready for what's next."

"Melissa Dawn Simkins bridges the worlds of elite athletics and executive leadership to show that the mindset, discipline, and preparation required to win on the court are the same qualities leaders must cultivate to perform when the stakes are high. In a time when organizations are navigating constant change and complexity, this work provides a practical and powerful framework for building leaders who can adapt, align their teams, and sustain performance."

"The Core 4 targets the leadership capacities that neuroscience proves are essential for sustained behavior change—agility, resilience, alignment, and well-being. It reflects the same mind-body connection we see in elite athletes: When leaders build both mental agility and physical resilience, they perform better under pressure."

"Melissa's hallmark has been redefining what effective leadership looks like under pressure. Her leadership conditioning system is not about motivation—it's about performance. The work we did together strengthened how I lead and directly supported my path to the CEO role."

AUDRA UPCHURCH, Chief Executive Officer,
Cybermedia Technologies

"*Athleadership* connects the inner and outer game of leadership in a way most frameworks miss. Melissa delivers real substance with clear business relevance. This is not a metaphor. It is a leadership system leaders can actually operate from and bring lasting change."

SUDHA SOLAYAPPAN, Vice President, Talent, Development &
Performance, PROCEPT BioRobotics

"*Athleadership* makes it crystal clear: Training installs skills, but conditioning becomes the operating system. Its reminder that mindset is the new skillset—and that elite leaders don't think faster, they recognize faster—is transformative."

RASHANDA HARRIS, Vice President, Enterprise Business Services
People Strategy & Corporate Services, LFG

"As AI accelerates decision velocity and reshapes how organizations operate, the advantage no longer lies in access to information but in the quality of human judgment under pressure. *Athleadership* reframes leadership as a performance discipline. It integrates insights from sport, neuroscience, and decision science into a framework that is both intellectually rigorous and operationally relevant. In AI-enabled environments defined by uncertainty and rapid change, this kind of conditioning is not optional. It is foundational to sustained performance."

SERGUEI NETESSINE, Senior Vice Dean for Innovation and Global
Initiatives, The Wharton School, University of Pennsylvania

"*Athleadership* is a framework for performance conditioning for business leaders. This is not inspiration or theory. It is a system that helps leaders build the mental and emotional discipline required when the stakes are real. I've seen firsthand how this mindset separates contenders from champions. *Athleadership* brings that edge to leadership."

RAPTI KHURANA, Former Vice President, Talent Engagement and
Development, National Football League

"Melissa Simkins brings clarity, authenticity, and real-world leadership insight in a way that truly resonates. Her recent Athleadership session with my leadership team at Truist was extremely well received—engaging, practical, and thought-provoking. The conversation left the team energized and wanting more. *Athleadership* reflects exactly what Melissa delivers: disciplined, human-centered leadership built for lasting impact."

FRED HILL, SVP, Digital Commerce and
Marketing Capabilities, Truist

"As a runner and former soccer player, I understood conditioning in sport but never connected it to leadership. Melissa helped me realize that leadership is not just about knowledge or intention; it is about conditioning how you think, show up, and lead others over time. That shift helped me translate my athletic mindset into how I lead people. The idea is simple, but the impact is lasting."

CHRIS SPALL, Behavioral Health Executive Director,
FL. UnitedHealth Group

"I've watched Melissa Dawn Simkins build movements that elevate leaders and create real momentum, from the She-Suite Summit to the evolution of Athleadership. She possesses a rare gift for convening and pushing leaders to rise to the moment they're called to lead. *Athleadership* is Melissa's masterclass: a distillation of everything she's built over years, helping leaders condition themselves to perform with clarity, courage, and purpose when it matters most."

DR. NICOLE F. ROBERTS, Founder and Chief Generosity Officer of Health & Human Rights Strategies and Author of *Generosity Wins*

ATH
LEAD
ER
SHIP

MELISSA DAWN SIMKINS

ATHLEADERSHIP

The Elite Athletic Mindset: *How to Lead Under Pressure and Perform When It Counts*

IDEAPRESS PUBLISHING

WASHINGTON, DC

IDEAPRESS
PUBLISHING

Ideapress Publishing | www.ideapresspublishing.com

All trademarks are the property of their respective companies.

Cover Design: Micah Kandros
Interior Design: Jessica Angerstein

Cataloging-in-Publication Data is on file with the Library of Congress.

Hardcover ISBN: 978-1-64687-250-3
eBook ISBN: 978-1-64687-330-2

Special Sales
Ideapress books are available at a special discount for bulk purchases for sales promotions and premiums, or for use in corporate training programs. Special editions, including personalized covers, a custom foreword, corporate imprints, and bonus content, are also available.

1 2 3 4 5 6 7 8 9 10

Glory to God,
who gave me the greatest gift—eternal life—
and entrusted me with this message.
To my husband and purpose partner, Will,
Thank you for being my constant in every season—I love you.
To Kevin, Shunn, and Amari—
may you rise to greatness in every way.
To my miracle, Kingston—
you are my greatest inspiration.
May you always see yourself as
the leader you were born to be.
To my family and front row—
Thank you for the encouragement every step of the way.
To every Athleader who refuses to shrink from the moment—
the builders and believers who rise.
Often counted on. Sometimes overlooked. But never counted out.
This is for you.
You are built from within.
Conditioned to win.

CONTENTS

Foreword by Michael Platt, PhD xv

PREFACE | Taking My Life Back.. xxi

PART I: WHY LEADERSHIP IS BREAKING

1 | Why the Old Playbook Can't Keep Up.................................1

2 | The Performance Paradox: The Silent Epidemic
Behind Success...13

3 | What's Missing Is Purpose in Practice, Not Just on Paper......33

PART II: THE ATHLEADERSHIP SYSTEM

4 | Introducing Athleadership 49

5 | Defining Your MVP—Mission, Vision, and Purpose 67

6 | Core 4: Because Conditioning Outperforms Training............89

7 | Agility: What to Do When the Ground Beneath You Shifts .. 107

8 | Resilience: Lose No Lessons 125

9 | Alignment: Purpose-Driven Performance 145

10 | Well-Being: Sustain Your Energy...163

PART III: FROM INSIGHT TO IMPACT

11 | The 90-Day Way: Make It Repeatable 183

12 | Scale the System: Build the Culture, Become
the Player-Coach.. 201

Acknowledgments 215

Glossary 217

Next Steps 221

Endnotes.. 223

Michael Platt, PhD

There are moments when everything tightens. We are living in one now.

As intelligence becomes increasingly artificial and access to information becomes ubiquitous, the value of information itself begins to flatten. The world is placing a different kind of demand on us—one that cannot be met with information alone, but only by how we show up.

The noise fades. Time compresses. The margin for error disappears. And whatever preparation you've done, or avoided, reveals itself all at once.

I learned early in life that in those moments, performance is not about what you know. It's about what you can summon.

I grew up in a home where uncertainty was constant. My dad was an auto mechanic who often worked two jobs, sometimes none. My mom worked a series of jobs before becoming a school bus driver while managing bipolar disorder under significant strain. We lived in a small home with little privacy, often unsure how bills would get paid. My father later developed cancer and died at 55. My wife and I financially supported my parents while still in training ourselves.

There was no playbook for navigating that kind of environment. What there was, however, was repeated exposure to pressure—and the need to keep moving forward anyway.

Sports was my proving ground.

I played football, baseball, and wrestled, eventually becoming captain of my high school football team. What I learned on the field was something I would only later understand scientifically: The edge does not come from talent alone. It comes from conditioning. From doing hard things repeatedly. From training your mind and body to stay focused, composed, and effective when everything in you wants to break.

Every athlete knows this. If you skip the hard work, you don't just fall behind—you lose access to your best self when it matters most. You see this at the highest levels of football. The difference between good and great quarterbacks is rarely information; they all know the playbook. It's who can stay composed when the pocket collapses, who can read the field and decide in seconds, under pressure, with everything on the line. That capacity isn't improvised in the moment. It's trained.

That lesson has stayed with me across every chapter of my life, from blue-collar small town to Ivy League culture shock and finally on to Wharton, and ultimately to a career studying how the brain drives decision-making, performance, and social connection.

At the Wharton Neuroscience Initiative I lead at the University of Pennsylvania, my colleagues and I study what differentiates high performers in the real world.

We began in sports, measuring how attention, emotion, and decision-making fluctuate during performance. The best athletes are not simply more skilled—they are better conditioned. Their attention is more stable, their responses more precise, and their recovery from mistakes faster.

What surprised us was how consistently these same principles appeared elsewhere.

In organizations, leadership potential is revealed not just in experience or personality, but in how individuals allocate attention, adapt strategies, and make decisions under uncertainty—patterns that emerge long before formal leadership roles.

In high-stakes environments like military operations, success similarly depends less on credentials and more on sustained focus, adaptability, and composure under pressure.

Across these contexts, a single pattern emerges:

Performance is not determined by what you know. It is determined by what you can summon under pressure.

What has been missing is a formal discipline to develop this capacity deliberately. What athletes have long understood as conditioning, leaders are only now beginning to recognize as essential. *Athleadership* represents that next frontier—a systematic approach to building the internal capacity required for modern leadership.

This insight has never been more important.

Artificial intelligence is rapidly reshaping the landscape of work. As intelligence becomes artificial, the premium shifts to what cannot be automated: judgment, trust, and the ability to act under uncertainty.

We are entering a brain economy, where cognitive, emotional, and social capacities—what we call brain capital—are the primary drivers of performance and value.

And yet, at precisely the moment these capacities matter most, leaders are struggling.

The pace of change has outstripped our ability to adapt. The human brain—built for a slower, smaller, simpler world—is now operating under constant strain. Attention fragments, emotional regulation falters, and decision-making degrades. This is not a failure of effort. It is a failure of conditioning.

This is where *Athleadership* comes in.

What Melissa Dawn Simkins offers is not another layer of tactics, but a fundamentally different approach: conditioning the leader from the inside out.

Her core insight—that leadership is less about what you do and more about how you are conditioned to show up—aligns closely with what we've learned from neuroscience. Under pressure, the brain does not rise to the level of knowledge. It falls back on trained patterns. If those patterns are reactive or fragmented, performance suffers. If they are stable and aligned, performance elevates.

Melissa's distinction between the external game and the internal arena captures this clearly. Most leaders focus on controlling the game: strategy, execution, outcomes. The most effective leaders invest in the arena, building the internal capacity to meet whatever the game demands.

This is the same principle that governs elite performance in sports, and it will define leadership in the age of AI.

There is a growing temptation to outsource effort. To rely on technology to think, analyze, and decide. But every athlete understands the cost of that instinct. If you fail to prepare, prepare to fail.

Technology can replace effort, but it cannot replace the benefits of effort.

Leadership is no different.

The future will belong to those who embrace the work of conditioning. Who train their minds to remain clear under pressure, regulate their emotions under stress, and align their actions with purpose in the face of uncertainty.

This is not about doing more. It is about becoming more.

More aware.

More adaptive.

More connected.

More resilient.

In my own work, I describe the "leader's brain" as the neural systems that enable connection, decision-making, and performance under pressure. These systems are not fixed. They can be strengthened through experience and deliberate practice. When they are, something remarkable happens: Teams synchronize, trust deepens, and performance rises—individually and collectively.

That is the promise of this book.

Athleadership offers a practical framework for developing the capacities that matter most now. It bridges the gap between knowing and doing, between potential and performance.

In a world where intelligence is increasingly artificial, this book shows you how to cultivate the one advantage that isn't: your ability to be fully human when it matters most.

—**MICHAEL PLATT,** Philadelphia, PA 2026
Director, Wharton Neuroscience Initiative
University of Pennsylvania

Taking My Life Back

I just want my life back. I didn't say that out loud for a long time, but the idea was the undercurrent to my everyday existence. It lurked under everything: my meetings, my makeup, the smile people assumed meant I was fine. The truth was simpler and heavier: I was losing myself.

For months, most mornings, I drove to the Marist High School track in Atlanta before sunrise. Before heading to work, I'd step out of my car with a gallon of water, drop my gym bag on the bleachers, and force my tired body into motion. I stretched, I sprinted, I ran stairs—again and again and again. In those early mornings, the scoreboard was dark, which seemed fitting because chasing wins had landed me there. At that point in my life, my personal scoreboard only measured volume. It ticked up an endless tally of more replies, more meetings, more hours— while clarity, joy, and wholeness were sidelined.

It didn't make sense to anyone—not even to me. Bills were piling up. Rent had to be paid. Contracts I depended on were unstable. New cli- ents needed to be courted. And yet there I was, conditioning for a body- building competition where I'd stand onstage in a bikini being judged on muscle tone and stage presence. It was an audacious goal when I could barely breathe financially. Predictably, an inner voice challenged my commitment: *Who do you think you are? You've never done anything like this. You can't be using your time to do this.* But I kept showing up, because something inside me knew the cost of staying the same. Something inside me knew I was disappearing. The grind had swallowed my identity. I had become the title, the role, the results. I was performing to achieve success defined by others but losing myself in the process.

To get my life back and regain my sense of self, I needed to build mental muscle. I invested in a bodybuilding coach; saved money by cutting back on dinners, shopping splurges, get-away trips; and met myself every day on that track. I lifted weights, focused on my nutrition, and slept eight hours each night. I followed this system five or six days a week for eight months. When my mom visited, she witnessed the level of discipline and daily conditioning it took to fully commit to this goal. It was costly but one of the most revealing experiences of my life. I finally put into words what I had been holding back for so long: "I'd become so consumed with work that I don't recognize myself anymore. I just want my life back."

One morning, as I sprinted off the starting line, my ring slipped from my finger and clinked onto the asphalt. It startled me, and was a sign that my body was changing faster than I had expected. Committing to a goal takes mental fortitude. For me, the hardest part was recalibrating my mindset. I had doubt, fear, and disbelief that had consumed my thinking for so long. Each day, I would condition my mindset by envisioning my transformation and declaring the outcome before it had become my reality. I would tell myself, "You can do this." The body was achieving what my mind had conceived. Looking back, that moment on the track was when I came back to myself. Sweat by sweat, mile by mile, I met pieces of myself I had buried—my discipline, my resilience, my joy, my strength, my inner athlete. The young woman who once danced, cheered, and believed hadn't left. I had just stopped listening to her.

Training for my first bodybuilding competition helped me reconnect with the athlete's mindset. My discipline paid off, and I took home second place in my first competition as a fitness athlete. But that win was bigger than a trophy. Along the journey, I'd discovered a new way to thrive.

If you've ever felt that, despite your success, you've lost your true self, you're not alone and you're not imagining it. This book is for the leader who has tasted success yet quietly senses the very real cost. It's for the leader who is outwardly respected but inwardly aware that the pace, pressure, or expectations have hollowed out something essential.

If you're looking for quick hacks, empty hype, or leadership shortcuts that avoid the deeper work, this book won't help you. But if you're hungry for true strength—to reclaim the parts of yourself you've misplaced, to lead from a deeper core, and to join a new league of leaders— then this offers you a new path. You can be who you are meant to be, and also be a leader who is built for pressure, purpose, and change.

The average professional spends 28 percent of their workday on email—before doing a minute of deep work.[1] We push, extend our days, and "just one more" ourselves into exhaustion. But that strategy cannot support the growth and productivity you need. After a point, our output drops, no matter how many hours we push ourselves.

When I realized I wanted my life back, I wasn't just speaking from a point of exhaustion. My soul was asking for air and a new daily rhythm. Practically, I had to face an uncomfortable truth: Overwork wasn't making me stronger; it was making me smaller. When I realized that, I reset the scoreboard. Instead of measuring my success in terms of hours, emails, meetings, and deadlines, I decided to track purpose-aligned performance. I was building myself for change.

The Real Problem: We're Not Conditioned for Uncertainty

The leadership story today tells us to do it all: scale, innovate, inspire, coach, hit the number, protect the culture, be emotionally intelligent—and somehow not burn out. We send leaders to workshops. We assign books. We provide them with mentors. But we don't condition them to navigate stress in real time. There's no simulation, no sustained feedback loop, and no system to metabolize high-pressure decisions and reset with purpose, presence, or values. It's like asking a quarterback to win the Super Bowl after watching three motivational videos and taking a competency assessment.

This isn't a realistic bar to set, especially when the world is changing so rapidly. The human brain isn't naturally wired to handle the velocity of constant disruption we are experiencing. It defaults to protection, not progression. We compensate with bravado, perfectionism, or over-performance. We compartmentalize instead of integrating. We try to control the chaos. We survive instead of aligning. But without a system of conditioning, we will fail.

This book doesn't want you to abandon high standards. My goal is to help you sustain your high performance without sacrificing your nervous system, your purpose, or your people. This is the work of inner conditioning:

- Know your identity built upon purpose, not just title or position.
- Build space between trigger and response.
- Align decisions with your purpose, not insecurity.
- Reclaim rest, presence, and boundaries as tools of peak performance.

This book is not about getting to the next level—it's about leading from a deeper one. **If we don't rewire our inner world, we are forced**

to react to change instead of leading it. *Athleadership* is the bridge that closes that gap by conditioning your mind and nervous system to move at the speed each moment requires. You don't need a bigger title. You need a deeper truth.

By fully aligning your individual purpose with your leadership approach, you can sustain high performance without the pressure to prove yourself. You can do it without quitting your dreams or abandoning excellence. To be clear, if you're running on the endless treadmill right now, you will slow down, whether you choose to or not. This isn't about slowing down to make life easier and become complacent with lower standards. It's about moving toward a place that sustains you—being powerful without being performative. Winning in a way that feels like winning. Being a successful leader without abandoning yourself in the process. This is how we return to purpose in practice and take our life back.

Leadership is played in two places: the game *outside* of you and the arena *within* you.

The game is the environment, the world—fast, unpredictable, constantly changing. It's everything that you cannot control.

By contrast, the arena is your internal mindset. You can control it so pressure meets preparation, so who you are meets what's required. This is where you strengthen your leadership from within.

Most leaders aren't struggling because the game is happening so fast. We're struggling because we never learned to condition our mindset. If you feel the weight of it—if you've been holding your breath or holding it together—I see you. More importantly, I want you to start seeing yourself.

This isn't just about healing burnout. It's about reawakening belief. Redefining success, not as something you chase but something you align with. True performance isn't about squeezing more out of yourself. It's about aligning your energy with what matters most. You don't need to prove your worth. You need to protect it.

Introducing Athleadership

If you're not in a season of disruption, one is headed your way. When the plan breaks, Athleadership can help you steady yourself, but you need to put in the work now to build the inner capacity you will need.

Athleadership is the performance operating system for modern leadership—built on the elite athletic mindset and designed to condition the mental and neurological capacities leaders rely on to perform under pressure, adapt through accelerating change, and stay anchored to purpose. It's a proven method rooted in neuroscience and performance psychology to rewire your mind so you can shift from feeling stuck to making a breakthrough.

The method is built on four key pillars:

 **Mission, vision, and purpose (MVP):** This pillar focuses on who you are because your identity becomes your compass. It helps you set your course, navigate challenges, and pursue your own vision of success.

 **The Core 4:** These four traits—agility, resilience, alignment, and well-being—help you stay on track and feel ready to rise to challenges. Together, the Core 4 act as your mental engine, giving you the drive to pursue your purpose.

 **Conditioning practice:** To develop strength, you need to condition your body, brain, and nervous system through repetition. The goal is to strengthen yourself without leaving you depleted. To do this, I'll guide you through reps, help you find your rhythm, and encourage you to make time for recovery.

This process will rewire your brain so you can become the person you want and need to be.

 **The 90-Day Way:** For change to be meaningful, it needs to be sustainable. That won't happen without effort, so the 90-Day Way becomes your quarterly action plan. Taking it season by season can help you increase your focus and avoid feeling overwhelmed.

Whether the world is calm or chaotic, pressure is always present. This gives you the capacity to meet any moment with clarity, purpose, and strength.

The power I gained on that track never left me. It became the quiet engine beneath every chapter of my life. I didn't sprint myself into a new season—I conditioned my mentality into a different kind of leadership. On that quiet track, I realized I wasn't just rebuilding my life but rebuilding myself. I was becoming the kind of leader my purpose required. That inner reconstruction became the foundation for the system you are now holding. And what I learned on that track was that the speed of change outside will always outpace the strength of a leader who isn't changing inside. What started as survival became my calling. In the two decades since then, life has reshaped me in ways I never planned. I found love after loss and became a wife. I became a mother, after being told the odds were slim. And I founded an award-winning, ed-tech leadership company that has influenced leaders across continents and transformed how organizations prepare their people for change.

Over the years, the individuals shaping business, sport, and influence have invited me into the conversations they cannot have publicly. I became their confidant, the person they call when the pressure is real, the stakes are high, and the external success no longer matches the internal strain. It is a sacred seat, earned by trust, consistency, and a relentless commitment to their growth.

Our methodology has been trusted by UBS Group AG (UBS), Procter & Gamble (P&G), Elevance Health, the National Football League (NFL), the National Basketball Association (NBA), world-class athletes, and Fortune 500 organizations committed to building leaders who can thrive under pressure. More than 250,000 leaders in over 25 countries have used this system to accelerate promotions, strengthen alignment, elevate performance, and rebuild confidence in seasons of disruption. Purpose, when activated consistently, becomes next-level performance.

What you will encounter in these pages is not theory. It is not recycled leadership speak. It is a discipline we pioneered—Athleadership—born from purpose, refined through practice, and validated across some of the world's most demanding environments. It has been proven by leaders who returned to their organizations with greater clarity, steadier decision-making, stronger teams, and measurable advancement in their careers. I work with C-suite leaders and those on the rise, helping them lead others without losing themselves, align identity with impact, and move from intention to execution with clarity and purpose. This is the discipline that turns purpose into performance—when it counts most.

Even now, I revisit the same operating system I will share with you and course correct. You never finish. You return. And every return sharpens you.

The Truth That Changed Everything

The Athleadership discipline validates what many already know: The same mindset that wins championships builds companies, transforms cultures, and carries you through pressure. When leaders fuse an elite athletic mindset with leadership mastery, something powerful happens. They become agile in strategy, resilient in adversity, aligned in purpose, and grounded in well-being. They become the people whom others trust when the moment demands them to rise.

The playing field of business may be unpredictable, but with Athleadership you're not bracing for impact; you're conditioning for it. I didn't know it back on that high school track, but every lap, every breath, every choice was preparing me—not just physically, but spiritually and mentally. It was identity work. It was the beginning of a new way of becoming a leader. And it revealed a truth to me: **Leaders aren't born. They're built—they are conditioned through change and under pressure.**

You don't need to be tapped on the shoulder or given a title to be a leader. A leader is anyone who chooses to take responsibility for their impact—someone with a vision compelling enough to move themselves and others toward something better. Leadership isn't about authority; it's about initiative. It's the decision to guide, to influence, to inspire— not because you must, but because you feel called to. If you've ever carried a moment that required courage, clarity, or direction; if you've ever been the person others look to when things get uncertain; if you've ever refused to let circumstances define your future, you're already leading. Leadership is a choice. And if you're reading this, you've likely already made it.

Now that you've seen my moment of truth, let's look at where so many of us find ourselves—and what it takes to move from surviving pressure to mastering it.

You've got this,

Melissa

Want to see how you perform under pressure? Take the Athleadership Pressure-Proof Assessment to get a snapshot of your leadership conditioning. Visit melissadawnsimkins.com/perform.

Why Leadership Is Breaking

The Case for a New Performance System

1

Why the Old Playbook Can't Keep Up

"The greatest danger in times of turbulence is not the turbulence; it is to act with yesterday's logic."

—Peter Drucker, Renowned management consultant and author

Standing in the airport terminal, at Gate C47, the email Marin had been waiting on finally arrived.

"We lost it."

She had moved through the day as leaders do when the stakes are high and the clock moves too fast: composed, practiced. She delivered direction, absorbed pressure, eased tensions, and made decisions. By noon, her voice had steadied three different rooms. By five, she had answered more questions than she had asked herself in a month.

Three words in bold at the top of the email thread, a verdict without ceremony: "We lost it."

She read it twice, not because she didn't understand, but because her body needed a moment to reconcile what her mind already knew: 14 months; a multinational partnership; a team that had sacrificed nights and weekends, vacations and birthdays; the kind of pursuit that steals something from you long before you realize it. Her breath tightened.

She scrolled.

A second sentence waited for her, quiet and devastating: "They said we couldn't move at their pace."

There it was, the truth she had been outrunning with precision and professionalism: The gap wasn't in her competence but in the system she had been trained to trust.

Around her, the terminal pulsed with the usual choreography of modern life—rolling suitcases, families in soft arguments, business travelers presenting as calm—while boarding-group numbers flickered on screens. Marin heard none of it. The noise fell away, replaced by a deeper kind of silence, the kind that arrives when the mind is forced to confront what the heart has sensed for too long: She hadn't failed. *The playbook had.*

Marin had followed the old rules with discipline: Plan thoroughly, communicate flawlessly, build consensus, anticipate resistance, steady the room. But as she closed her eyes in that fluorescent air terminal, her body told the truth her training could not protect her from: She had been playing a modern game with an ancient playbook. And the game had finally outrun the rules.

But Marin noticed something shifting inside her. Her chest softened. A strange calm settled in. For the first time in years, she wasn't telling herself to fix it or force it or frame it as a lesson. This was *new*.

Marin opened her eyes, the terminal snapping back into motion around her. Nothing had changed—and yet everything had. A sentence rose within her, uninvited but honest: *I'm not broken. The model is.* It was the first moment of real clarity she'd had in years. It did more than adjust her path; it was preparing her for an entirely different way of leading.

The Leadership System Is Outdated

The leadership model Marin inherited, and perhaps you did as well, was engineered for a world that no longer exists, and yet we continue to cling to it as though it still possesses the power to carry us into the future. For decades, the prevailing wisdom taught us that leadership was a linear journey—one you could ascend through discipline, mastery, and a certain polished composure: Read the book, attend the workshop, take the assessment, review the slide deck. But the world shifted with a velocity that the old playbook simply couldn't anticipate. New technologies dissolved boundaries, global crises compressed timelines, and cultural expectations reshaped what people needed from leaders. While the environment accelerated, the system designed to develop leaders stayed anchored to rituals from a slower era. The old playbook taught us that pausing for reflection was a luxury reserved for quiet seasons, decision-making was a function of control rather than clarity, and performance was something to be achieved through sheer force of will.

The problem is not a lack of intelligence or motivation; it is the mismatch between the pace of modern change and the pace of human development.

Leaders today are operating in environments that move in spirals, shocks, and surges, while the systems that shape them still imagine step-by-step choreography and predictable outcomes. The old model subtly convinces you that if you just try harder, stay longer, or care more, you can outrun the pressure. And when you inevitably falter, the struggle feels personal rather than structural.

But here is the truth most leadership literature still whispers around rather than naming boldly: The greatest risk inside modern organizations is not weak strategy or market volatility—it is leaders whose internal systems are cracking beneath the weight of the inevitable instability of rapid change and pressure.

These fractures rarely present themselves in dramatic ways. Instead, they show up in moments so subtle they are easy to miss: a hesitation during a decision that used to feel instinctive, a quiet withdrawal from conversations that once energized you, a performance that remains outwardly steady while your inner clarity begins to thin. Pressure doesn't always roar. Sometimes it whispers. Sometimes it erodes.

If you've ever felt yourself speeding internally—your mind racing ahead, your nervous system firing warnings, your clarity trailing behind—you've experienced this mismatch firsthand. It is not a sign that you are incapable. It is a sign that you are attempting to move at a pace your system was never conditioned to sustain.

Behind strategies, spreadsheets, and KPIs is a biological truth we've ignored for far too long: You were not designed to live at war with your own pace. As researcher and author Brené Brown shared at a *Fortune* magazine conference, American workers are not neurologically wired for this level of rapid change and instability: "People are not okay."[2]

Your brain was not wired for unending surveillance.

Your nervous system was not crafted for perpetual acceleration.

Your identity was never meant to be fused to your output.

The old model demanded leaders outrun their biology, override their humanity, and mute their intuition in the name of performance. It assumed leaders would remain composed through storms they were never conditioned to navigate. It taught them to push past exhaustion, obscure their limitations, and conceal their instability behind professional polish. And when it all begins to feel impossible—as it has for so many leaders across industries, cultures, and generations—we misdiagnose the problem as a personal flaw rather than a systemic failure. We quietly question our competence when the truth is far simpler and far more liberating: It's not you that's breaking. It's the playbook.

Marin's moment at Gate C47 was not merely a professional disappointment; it was an awakening. It revealed the silent fracture between what modern leadership demands and what traditional development prepares us to handle. Her clarity—arriving in the hum of an airport terminal—was not the product of failure but the first signal that the system she had trusted for years could no longer sustain the reality she was navigating.

This is not a call for leaders to speed up. It is a call to evolve the inner architecture that allows you to remain centered, strategic, and whole as the world around you accelerates. The invitation is not to run harder, but to see more honestly; not to adapt more frantically, but to evolve more intentionally; not to squeeze more resilience out of a system that was never designed to protect you, but to build a new one that finally does. That begins with telling the truth without flinching: Leaders aren't failing the world. The world has outrun the model that shaped them.

The Equation That Quietly Reshaped Leadership

Marin stood in the center of the airport walkway. The loss of the deal hurt, but the client's assessment—"we couldn't move at their pace"—put into words what her body had been whispering for months. The speed of the environment had outpaced the speed of her conditioning. What Marin was experiencing in that brightly lit terminal was not personal failure but the mathematical truth of the modern world—a truth so simple and so devastating that most leaders never fully acknowledge it.

The speed and complexity of change (C) was greater than the speed and depth of development (D). As a simple equation,

$$C > D$$

Change today moves on a curve that keeps steepening—market shifts, geopolitical voltage, digital acceleration, AI disruption, cultural reorientation, economic volatility—while our ability to adapt, process, integrate, and respond is still governed by a nervous system built for slower terrain. Leaders feel this mismatch without always having the language for it. We call it anxiety, overwhelm, burnout, fog, fatigue, imposter syndrome, and loss of clarity. **But beneath every name is the same equation, meaning the internal architecture has not been conditioned for the velocity of external demands.**

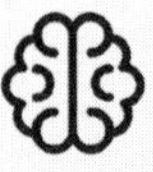 Neuroscience confirms what leaders sense but rarely articulate: The human brain processes information in linear increments, but the world is delivering inputs in exponential waves. Under pressure, the amygdala, the brain's threat detection center, activates faster than the prefrontal cortex can regulate.

When change accelerates beyond our capacity to metabolize it, cognition narrows, emotional regulation thins, and decision-making becomes a high-wire act performed on a frayed rope. This is not a character flaw. It is biology colliding with velocity.

When a leader like Marin feels behind, scattered, or stretched beyond reason, it isn't because she lacks discipline or drive. It's because she is operating inside an equation she never consented to, one that practically guarantees internal overload. C > D, development not keeping up with change, is not a commentary on competence but on design. And until leaders have a new operating model that closes the gap, no amount of striving will keep pace with the speed of the world they're asked to navigate. Leaders do not rise to the level of their knowledge; they fall to the level of their conditioning. And when the world is changing faster than we can integrate, leaders end up performing at the edge of their identity with no internal scaffolding to hold them.

This is why exhaustion has become the quiet undertone of modern work. According to research by Censuswide, 66 percent of American employees experienced some sort of burnout in 2025, but the kind of conditioning we'll explore in the Athleadership approach can help them heal.[3]

Marin's nervous system could no longer pretend everything was aligned. Working harder doesn't work. Instead, leaders must evolve.

This moment doesn't need leaders who hustle harder; it needs leaders working with a new operating system. And that system requires inner conditioning to metabolize pressure instead of being destabilized by it. Athleadership rewires a leader's identity beyond their job title so they can stay aligned when the ground shifts. This new system is not bound by the limits of C > D, so it's capable of closing the gap from the inside out. Where the old equation fails, a new one begins.

Marin didn't have this language yet, but her intuition was catching up to her reality. She understood that the old ways of leading had reached their limit, and something new would be required of her.

What Neuroscience Confirms

Long before leaders began naming their exhaustion, the brain understood that we were never built for this speed. Neuroscience does not indict us; it reveals us to ourselves.

For most of human history, the brain's primary assignment was survival, not performance. Its finest engineering was devoted to detecting threats, preserving energy, and maintaining homeostasis. Safety, not innovation. Certainty, not reinvention. The neural architecture that governs your leadership—the prefrontal cortex that handles strategy, emotional regulation, empathy, sequencing, and executive decision-making —is exquisitely powerful, but exquisitely fragile under pressure. When the pace of demands exceeds the pace of processing, the brain defaults to shortcuts, instinct, and defense rather than clarity, creativity, or courageous action. This is why the modern leadership environment feels so disorienting. You have the right capabilities, but your biology is being stretched beyond its original blueprint. Neuroscience research shows that chronic stress weakens connectivity within the prefrontal cortex and executive control, biasing neural processing away from higher-order regulation and toward more reactive, survival-oriented circuitry.[4] Leaders interpret this shift as "stress," "overwhelm," or "mental fog," but at a biological level, it is something far more fundamental: neural circuits prioritizing survival over strategy.

The speed of change is not just a corporate challenge but a cognitive one. The brain processes new information by creating mental models that predict what will happen next. But when the environment changes faster than those models can update, the brain experiences what neuroscientists call cognitive overload, a state where incoming data exceeds the brain's capacity to sort, filter, and integrate. It's the same phenomenon that causes a computer to freeze when too many tabs are open—the system isn't broken; it's overwhelmed.

And then there is pressure, the invisible force multiplier modern leaders underestimate most. Research shows that under acute stress, even highly skilled leaders lose access to the neural pathways associated with complex reasoning and future-focused thinking.[5] In its place emerges reactive decision-making: tunnel vision, snap judgments, and emotional reactivity disguised as efficiency. You may still look composed on the outside, but internally the system is rerouting, scrambling, and conserving. This is why leaders often describe the sensation of being on, yet not fully present; responsible for everything, yet connected to nothing; moving faster than ever, yet unable to feel like they are getting ahead. It is not incompetence. It is neurobiology.

Here is the truth I need you to hear with clarity and compassion: You are not failing; your wiring is firing exactly as designed. The mismatch is between the world you are leading in and the brain you are leading with. Once you see this, the shame falls away and possibility enters.

As we explore this model, you'll discover that although you can't bully the brain into higher performance, you can condition it. You can strengthen its capacity for clarity under pressure. You can build neural pathways that stay open even when the environment destabilizes. You can become the kind of leader whose presence calms the room precisely because your inner world is conditioned, not just informed.

That's Athleadership.

Training tells you what to do, while conditioning transforms who you become under pressure. And neuroscience makes this unmistakably clear: Leaders who do not condition their inner system will always be outpaced by the system around them. Conversely, leaders who learn to work with their wiring to harness the brain's plasticity, adaptive potential, and capacity to build strength under strain become rarer, steadier, and highly valued in a world that refuses to slow down. They become the ones who can lead where others freeze. They become the leaders whose identity stays anchored even when the environment destabilizes.

They become Athleaders.

When the Playbook Breaks in Real Life

Marin was beginning to make meaning of what she'd sensed but hadn't yet had the language for until the lightbulb came on when she read that email. And as she continued to process it, she began to realize that because the world was accelerating faster than her organization's internal system could support, something needed to change.

Thankfully, her team trusted her not simply because she delivered results but because she carried a kind of internal choreography: steady voice, precise thinking, calm presence. She was the leader who made the impossible look like Tuesday.

Marin had the instincts of an Athleader and was ready to begin to do things differently.

As she began to recognize the real cost of the old playbook, she was willing to move forward, and to lead her team, in a new way.

In the moment when the old rules stopped working, when effort was no longer enough, the critical decision Marin made was simply to be open to changing herself, her style, to meet the demands of a world that is not slowing down. This is the genesis of an Athleader, someone who performs under pressure and adapts through change.

Where the Old Playbook Ends and Conditioning Begins

When Marin finally sank into her window seat and the cabin lights dimmed around her, she felt a fatigue that wasn't physical at all. It was the kind that settles in the soul after years of sprinting in a world that keeps moving the finish line. She didn't open her laptop. She didn't study the loss. She didn't rehearse what she would say to her team. Instead, she allowed the stillness, a rare and unscripted pause, to reveal what the noise of her life had been drowning out. For the first time, she realized that the old playbook had trained her in the topics of leadership, but it had not prepared her for the conditions of leading in the modern world. It had taught her how to communicate but not how to stay regulated while doing it, how to make decisions but not how to quiet the noise so clarity could rise, and how to perform but not how to remain whole while performing.

What Marin most needed was a system that could carry her humanity and her intellect through the storm. She needed a rhythm that honored recovery as much as output and a framework that helped her stay aligned when the ground moved.

The insights we have today about neurobiology tell us that the leaders who thrive next won't be the ones who know the most: They'll be the ones who are conditioned the best. That doesn't mean they're conditioned to endure more; it means that they'll collapse less. They'll understand and honor their limits. They'll recover in rhythm.

This new playbook is rooted not in performance alone but in purpose, identity, rhythm, recovery, emotional clarity, and mental muscle. It's a system that helps leaders rise when pressure peaks. It's a model built for change, not undone by it.

As the plane lifted and the city dissolved into a scatter of lights beneath her, Marin was ready to embrace a new way of operating. As she did, something in her exhaled for the first time in months, as if releasing a truth she had been holding for far too long: *The system doesn't need a stronger version of me. It needs a different kind of me.* And that shift—subtle, seismic—marked the beginning of a new way of leading that would demand more honesty, more alignment, and more courage than anything she had been trained to do before.

2

The Performance Paradox: The Silent Epidemic Behind Success

"Define success on your own terms, achieve it by your own rules, and build a life you're proud to live."

—Anne Sweeney, Former president of Disney Channel

We are living through an era where leaders look strong on the outside but are quietly breaking on the inside—and almost no one is naming what's happening. The greatest crisis in modern leadership is not incompetence or indifference or even instability; it is the quiet unraveling that occurs when the excellence everyone can see no longer matches the inner architecture required to sustain it. That gap—between outward success and inward depletion—is what I call the Performance Paradox.

The Performance Paradox is the condition of being rewarded for the very behavioral patterns that erode your identity. You are praised and promoted for behaviors that slowly break your sense of self, until external success and internal reality no longer resemble one another. You look like you're winning, yet something essential in you is eroding, and the applause becomes both reward and anesthetic. Performance brings us rewards, but if we don't approach it systematically, it can also entrap us.

The Paradox rarely announces itself as a single dramatic collapse. It accrues in small compromises: the vacation you cancel because the deal "can't close without you," the boundary you quietly move because someone else drops the ball, the conversation you avoid because telling the truth might disturb the peace. Over time, performance stops being something you do and becomes something you feel compelled to prove. You're no longer simply executing at a high level; you're fighting to protect an identity that has fused itself to output.

Most high achievers misinterpret this erosion. They read their exhaustion as evidence of weakness, when in reality it is evidence of misalignment. They are carrying levels of pressure their internal system has not been conditioned to hold. Their bodies and brains are telling the truth long before their mouths are willing to form the words. Research on burnout, disengagement, and workplace stress has moved from the margins to the center; it now defines the landscape.[6] Across industries, leaders report rising levels of chronic fatigue, emotional exhaustion, and quiet quitting.[7] Many live on the edge most days—with little space to recover—while still delivering results that make others confuse their survival for strength.

If you find yourself stretched thin, hollowed out, or unsure who you are when the performance stops, hear this clearly: You are not failing or fragile. You are experiencing the predictable outcome of a paradox that has shaped an entire era of high performers.

The Performance Paradox is the condition of being rewarded for the very behavioral patterns that erode your identity.

In Quiet Rooms

Darren was the kind of leader organizations quietly build contingency plans around. When projects went sideways, his name was the one spoken with relief. In tense meetings, he could lower the temperature of the room with a single measured sentence. His peers described him as steady, composed, dependable—the person who would never drop the ball, never raise his voice, never let anyone see the strain. What they didn't see was how much of himself he had spent constructing that calm. The day his inner world began to fracture did not arrive with catastrophe. It arrived on an ordinary Thursday, under fluorescent light, in a ninth-floor conference room that carried the faint, burnt smell of coffee. Darren slid into his usual seat with his usual preparation—notes in order, posture intentional, expression open but guarded. His performance armor was zipped all the way to his throat.

Midway through the meeting, his division president looked up from the agenda with the ease of someone who assumes capacity is limitless. "Darren, I want you to lead point on the acquisition," he said. "We need you to stabilize the transition. Consider it your top priority."

The room nodded, already moving mentally to the next line item. Darren didn't. Before his mind could assemble a single conscious thought, his body answered for him. A tightening under his ribs. A high, insistent ringing in his left ear. A sudden awareness of fatigue that felt less like being tired and more like having the floor quietly drop an inch beneath his feet. In that split second, he watched his long-promised vacation with his wife—the trip postponed twice, the one she had circled on the calendar as if circling hope itself—evaporate.

"Darren?" his president asked again, this time with a hint of expectation. "Are you good with that?" There were eyes on him now, waiting for his predictably calm assent—the one that kept the machine moving and confirmed, yet again, that he could be counted on. He nodded. He said yes. He rescued the moment. And somewhere inside him, something essential cracked.

From the outside, nothing changed. His slide decks remained immaculate. His tone retained its measured confidence. His team continued to lean on him as the steady center of their storm. But beneath the surface, his nervous system had crossed a threshold. His sympathetic system—already over-recruited by years of "I'll handle it"—surged like an alarm. His heart rate climbed. His breathing shallowed. His cognitive bandwidth narrowed to a sharp, anxious tunnel. What he experienced as tightness and ringing was his body sending a message his identity wouldn't yet allow him to speak: *You cannot keep performing like this without consequence.*

Over the following weeks, the unraveling was almost invisible. His performance metrics held. The feedback from senior leaders remained glowing. Yet his sleep splintered into short, restless fragments. He woke clenched, as if he had spent the night bracing for impact. His appetite thinned. He felt constant panic—once a rare visitor—beginning to loiter in the margins of his days, pressing on his chest in the elevator, shortening his breath before town halls, slipping in just as he reached for the conference room door—always with just enough time to smooth his face before he stepped into view.

This is the cruel logic of the Performance Paradox: The suffering intensifies in the same season the success becomes most visible. The higher you climb, the less room you feel you have to tell the truth about how much it costs you to stay there. **Psychologists have a term for what was happening inside Darren. They call it identity foreclosure—a state in which a person's sense of self narrows so tightly around a single role or pattern of performance that any threat to that role feels like a threat to their very existence.**[8] Darren wasn't simply afraid of the workload; he was afraid of what it would mean about who he was if he said no, if he faltered, if he let someone else carry the ball for once. His "yes" was less about opportunity and more about survival.

His world did not explode. It quietly shrank. The Saturday golf rounds that had once been nonnegotiable began to slip off his calendar, replaced by "just this one" working session. His friends, who had grown used to his last-minute cancellations and distracted presence, stopped pressing. "We figured you'd be swamped," one of them said, not unkindly, when they ran into each other months later. The group text still pinged on weekend mornings, but no one really expected him to show up. At home, his wife tried to find him behind the glass of his fatigue. "Are you here," she asked one evening, "or just in the room?" He smiled, made a small joke, and shut his laptop for an entire 20 minutes before reopening it once she went to bed.

The erosion was not just emotional; it was physical. His blood pressure climbed. His doctor nudged his medication upward. His shoulders stayed locked in a permanent half-flinch. Still, the recognition plaques on his office wall multiplied, and the organization continued to quietly organize itself around his capacity. By the time he realized how far he had drifted from himself, the distance between who he appeared to be and who he felt himself becoming was so wide it seemed uncrossable.

Darren's story might not be yours in its details, but you may recognize its shape. Your triggering moment may have been a restructuring, a board review, a layoff announcement, a missed milestone, a crisis at home, the weight of being the only one like you in the room, or the subtle pressure of always being the person who can "handle it." The settings differ. The cast shifts. But the pattern remains hauntingly similar.

When performance becomes the container for identity, pressure stops being situational. It becomes existential. Every ask feels like a referendum on who you are allowed to be. The Performance Paradox convinces you that exhaustion is the price of excellence, when in truth, exhaustion is the tax on misalignment.

The Silent Epidemic of Identity Theft

Long before burnout shows up on a medical chart, and long before a resignation letter hits a leader's desktop, something far quieter begins to unfold beneath the surface of a life. **Identity does not disappear overnight; it is slowly bargained away in exchange for belonging, approval, stability, and status.** What begins as a strength—the willingness to show up, to be counted on, to exceed expectations—gradually becomes a script that leaves little room for your full self to exist.

From the earliest years, many of us internalized a straightforward equation: Perform well, be praised; fall short, be corrected. High grades, clean report cards, goals scored, solos sung, roles in the school play— these became the metrics by which adults signaled pride and affection. Purpose, inner conviction, and emotional truth rarely receive that same spotlight. We learned, long before we had language for it, that excellence equaled acceptance and reliability equaled safety.

By the time we step into our first professional roles, an astonishing amount of who we are has already been shaped by expectations we never consciously chose. We become fluent in reading the room, adapting our tone, stretching our capacity, and anticipating needs before they are voiced. In many ways, those skills serve us. They open doors. They build trust. They put us in rooms we once only imagined. **But without an**

internal system to protect identity, the same instincts that elevate us can begin to erase us.

I know this not just as a confidant to influential leaders, but as a woman who has lived it. I remember sitting in a room I had every reason to feel at home in—a room curated for experts in leadership, sport, and culture to discuss the future of performance. My work and my team's work had helped shape the very conversation on the agenda. Still, when the focus shifted to me, an old reflex rose like muscle memory. I began to edit myself while speaking. I softened statements I knew were firm. I framed my contributions with "we," even when the insight had been forged in the quiet of my own lived experience. I shrank by degrees, not because I lacked conviction but because somewhere along the way I had learned that my full presence carried a cost.

After the session, one of the leaders in the room approached me and said, with a clarity that felt like both compliment and confrontation, "I have a feeling you were sitting there thinking, 'I'm light-years ahead on this.'" She wasn't trying to flatter me. She was naming what she could see: I was moderating myself to keep the room comfortable. Her words pierced because they landed on an old wound. Years earlier, in different environments, I had been explicitly taught to dim my light. Use *we*, not *I*. Don't be too strong, too direct, too certain. Make your brilliance easier to digest. Present your leadership as a collective effort, so no one feels threatened by your individual contribution. Those messages had wrapped themselves around my nervous system so thoroughly that shrinking felt not only familiar but responsible.

That is how identity theft works at the level of the soul. Not with a dramatic announcement, but with micro-surrenders that seem wise in the moment: a softened opinion here, a withheld truth there, a slightly smaller posture when the moment actually requires the full force of your presence. You become smaller to belong and, in the process, abandon essential parts of who you were born to be. This is identity foreclosure in real time. You commit to a narrow version of yourself—the reliable one, the fixer, the polite disruptor who never disrupts too much—and arrange your life around upholding that version. On the surface, you appear composed, even enviable. Internally, you are brittle because the self you bring to the world rests on pillars that can be pulled away: a job title, a company's favor, a leader's endorsement, a team's dependence, a platform's validation.

Research on burnout and emotional exhaustion consistently shows that high performers are particularly vulnerable, not because they lack resilience but because their identity has become entangled with their role.[9] At every level, the Performance Paradox has widespread implications. When the role shakes, the self shakes. When the scoreboard dips, worth feels at risk. **Leaders think they are tired because they are doing too much, when in reality they are tired because they are not spending enough time being themselves.** The world rarely names this erosion. It simply keeps rewarding the version of you that is most useful to it. Your availability is praised as dedication. Your lack of boundaries is interpreted as passion. Your emotional labor is romanticized as "servant leadership," even when it is draining you.

The good news—and the hard news—is that this realization is not the end of the story. It is the beginning of awakening. Once you can see the pattern, once you have language for what has been happening inside of you, autopilot begins to lose its grip. The part of you that has been buried under expectation begins to stir. That stirring is not rebellion; it is remembrance. It is your identity tracing its way back to the surface.

Why We Overperform: What Neuroscience Reveals

If all of this were just a mindset problem, you could fix it with a better planner, a weekend away, or a new affirmation on the bathroom mirror, but the Performance Paradox is not simply a bad habit. It is a pattern etched into your nervous system, reinforced by both your story and your surroundings. To understand why it is so difficult to step out of overperformance, even when you know it is harming you, we have to acknowledge what is happening in your brain and body.

High achievers do not overperform because they are careless or undisciplined. They overperform because somewhere along the way, their brain learned to confuse performance with safety.[10] It is a pattern that can stem from childhood, where our worth was conditional on achievement.

Now, today, every time you took on more than was healthy and the crisis passed, your nervous system took note. Every time you rescued a failing project and were praised for it, your brain filed that pattern as protective. Every time you said yes when you meant no and avoided conflict, your body breathed a brief sigh of relief. These moments create a loop: overextension followed by temporary peace, depletion followed by external approval.[11] The loop teaches your survival system: This is what keeps us safe. Do it again.

Over time, those loops harden into identity. Not just in language—*I'm the one who always comes through*—but in neural circuitry. The brain becomes efficient at what it repeats. It builds pathways around the behaviors that seem to preserve stability. You stop simply doing more and start feeling like you must be more: more capable, more available, more in control. 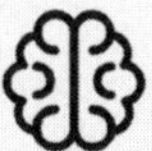

This is why change—even change you consciously want—can feel so destabilizing. A new leader arrives, your role shifts, a merger changes the rules, your children enter a new life stage, your parent's health declines, your own body introduces new limits. These events don't just alter your calendar; they shake the scaffolding of the self you've built around being competent and in command.

In those moments, the brain does what it was wired to do long before you ever held a title. The amygdala, your internal alarm system, begins scanning for danger.[12] Stress hormones like cortisol and adrenaline flood your system, preparing you to fight, flee, or freeze. Blood flow shifts away from the prefrontal cortex—the part of your brain you rely on for creative problem-solving, empathy, and nuanced judgment—toward the regions that manage immediate threat.[13] You may experience this as racing thoughts, a tightening chest, irritability, or a sudden difficulty concentrating. But beneath those sensations is a simpler, more primal question than any on your to-do list: *Are we safe?*

For a brain that has equated overperformance with protection, "safe" doesn't mean aligned; it means familiar and controllable. Delegation feels risky because it threatens the narrative that you are the one who holds things together. Rest feels irresponsible because it interrupts the cycle of doing that has shielded you from deeper questions. Saying no feels like standing at the edge of a cliff, even when the rational part of you knows the choice is reasonable.

Under sustained stress, the brain tends to default to the most practiced patterns, even when those patterns are harmful. Chronic pressure erodes flexibility. You become more rigid, not because you lack capacity, but because your biology is trying to reduce uncertainty.

This is what cognitive overload looks like in real life: Your brain is processing so many demands and potential threats that it starts closing tabs—not the urgent ones, but the human ones—empathy, creativity, patience. You're still meeting deadlines, but you've misplaced your joy, your curiosity, your ability to truly see the people you lead.

This is why leaders who are brilliant under clear conditions can feel disoriented when life asks them to reinvent themselves. They have built skill but not identity capacity. They have been trained in strategy but not conditioned in self-leadership. They can perform, but they cannot rest inside that performance. They can execute, but they cannot locate the self that exists apart from execution.

And yet, nestled inside this sobering reality, is profound hope. The same science that explains the Paradox offers a path forward. The brain is not fixed; it is pliable. Neural pathways can weaken when they are no longer rehearsed and strengthen when new patterns are repeated. Identity is not static; it is formed and reformed through experience, meaning, and practice.

This is where Athleadership begins to distinguish itself from traditional leadership assumptions. Training alone gives you information. Conditioning reshapes your identity. Conditioning teaches your nervous system how to stay grounded when the familiar dissolves, how to tolerate uncertainty without gripping for control, how to move through pressure with presence rather than panic. Athletes know this intuitively. Their season is built around deliberately stepping into stress so the body can adapt, recover, and return stronger. Athleaders can develop their own system of conditioning, repetition, and recovery.

Consider the story of Charlie Batch. Raised in a Pittsburgh community knit together by steel, grit, and belief, he left home to chase his dream of playing quarterback at the highest level. While he was in college, his younger sister, Danyl, was killed when she was used as a human shield in a senseless act of violence. There are moments that shatter identity so completely that the brain does not know where to file them. This was one of those moments.

Charlie could have collapsed under the weight of grief. Many would have. But the habits that had shaped him as an athlete—the discipline of showing up, the repetition of fundamentals, the ability to convert pain into preparation—gave his nervous system a different script. He did not bypass the pain; he learned to metabolize it. Eventually, he returned to Pittsburgh as a quarterback for the Steelers, bringing home not just a contract and two Super Bowl rings, but a mission. Through the Best of the Batch Foundation, he and his wife, Tasha, now invest in thousands of young people in neighborhoods like the one that once threatened to take everything from him.

Charlie did not simply survive tragedy. He rewired it into purpose. That transformation did not happen in a single leap. It was built over time, through repeated choices to align his actions with a deeper "why." That is neuroplasticity in motion. That is identity refusing to be defined solely by pain and performance. That is the kind of conditioning leaders need to withstand the pressures of modern work without losing themselves. You cannot outhustle an overactive survival system.

> *"Without the loss of my sister, which tested my resilience, I can't tell you we would be servicing thousands of kids through our educational programs at Best of the Batch Foundation."*
>
> —CHARLIE BATCH, Founder, Best of the Batch Foundation, 2x NFL Super Bowl Champion

You cannot outperform a misaligned identity. But you can rewire both. Overperformance is your nervous system trying to keep you safe. Alignment is the signal to your whole system that you already are.

The Culture That Rewards
Your Exhaustion

Of course, none of this happens in a vacuum. If your nervous system provides the internal architecture for the Performance Paradox, culture provides the scaffolding that keeps it standing. From the classroom to the boardroom, we are steeped in environments that normalize depletion and romanticize self-sacrifice.

As children, many of us were praised for pushing through fatigue, for being "low-maintenance," for not needing attention. In school, we learned that the hardest-working students—not necessarily the most grounded ones—were held up as examples. In sports, pain was framed as proof of commitment. By the time we arrive in career life, the vocabulary of worth is already familiar: busy, driven, tireless.

Organizations, often unintentionally, amplify these scripts. The leaders who respond to late-night emails are sometimes viewed as committed. The ones who quietly absorb additional work are labeled team players. Promotions often go to those who can carry the heaviest load the longest, not necessarily to those who are most aligned, most whole, or most capable of leading others into sustainable performance. Many companies now publish values about well-being and balance, yet the cultural norms still whisper a different rule: Show me your sacrifice, and I'll show you your value.

In this kind of ecosystem, the behaviors that harm you are the very ones that can earn you praise. Your longer hours are admired. Your blurred boundaries are applauded. Your tendency to always say yes is interpreted as loyalty. Your emotional labor—holding everyone's anxiety, smoothing conflict, mentoring those who are struggling—is called "natural leadership," even when it is pulling energy from a well that is nearly dry.

The system, in other words, affirms the version of you that costs you the most.

Engagement is collapsing, and the crisis at work often starts from the top. Recent research shows that more than a quarter of leaders have considered quitting in the past year, and a large percentage would give up their title just to feel engaged again.[14] That is a stunning signal that something matters more than status. Leaders are telling us that the old way of performing is no longer sustainable.

The collapse, when it comes, is rarely theatrical. It arrives in the slow erosion of things that once mattered deeply: the friendships you have no energy to maintain, the creative pursuits you keep promising yourself you'll return to, the spiritual or reflective practices that get crowded out by one more urgent request. It shows up in the moment you close your laptop at midnight and realize you cannot remember the last time you felt joy without also feeling guilt. And yet, the next morning, you log back in. You do what the system has trained you to do: swallow your fatigue, push past your frustration, put on your game face, and perform.

This cultural layer of the Performance Paradox matters because it helps you see that your struggle is not just personal; it is systemic. You are not the only one trying to stay human in a machine that rewards numbness. Naming that reality doesn't absolve us of responsibility, but it does free us from shame. The problem is not that you are weak. The problem is that the rules of the game were never designed for wholeness. What the world rewards is not always what makes you well. What the culture applauds is not always what makes you strong. What the system values is not always what makes you whole. Naming that truth is the first act of liberation. The next is even braver: choosing to live by a different standard.

Who's to Blame?

Let me be clear about something that often gets misunderstood in conversations like this: The organization is not the enemy, and pressure is not the problem. In every organization I've partnered with—from Fortune 500 companies to global sports organizations—the breakthrough moments have come when leaders learned how to align who they are with how they lead. That alignment didn't just transform the individual; it transformed the culture.

Companies want leaders who are whole, grounded, and fully alive in their purpose—because those leaders make better decisions, cultivate healthier teams, and deliver more sustainable results. **But most organizations simply don't have an operating system that teaches leaders how to build themselves from the inside out. They reward output because it's visible; they rarely invest in identity because it's invisible.**

When leaders operate from alignment rather than fear, teams experience a ripple effect: lower stress, increased trust, greater creativity, and measurably better decision quality. Alignment is not soft; it is a performance advantage. This means you need an operating model that teaches you how to anchor your identity so your performance is fueled by alignment, not depletion. When identity leads and performance follows, the organization benefits: lower turnover, higher engagement, stronger resilience under change, and a culture built on clarity rather than survival.

The Performance Paradox doesn't result in only a personal wound; it creates an organizational blind spot. Athleadership gives both the leader and the organization a shared language to heal both. It is not a rebellion against work; it is a return to purposeful work. It is a system that protects the leader and advances the mission, while also helping the individual rise and the organization win. It makes you more powerful, not less compliant; more effective, not less ambitious; more grounded, not less driven. You don't have to choose between your success and yourself. That is the shift from performing for your role to being powered by your purpose.

Across more than 400 leaders from 11 countries and multiple organizations, a strikingly consistent pattern emerged. Titles, industries, and geographies varied—but the internal experience did not.

These leaders were capable, accomplished, and deeply invested in their roles. Yet many described operating in a near-constant state of urgency—making decisions faster, but with less clarity, carrying increasing responsibility without sufficient recovery. Pressure was no longer episodic. It had become ambient.

What surfaced most clearly was not a lack of talent, motivation, or effort. It was a widening gap between what leaders were being asked to carry and the internal capacity available to carry it well. Purpose existed in aspiration but too often failed to translate into daily decisions when pressure was highest.

The Paradox was no longer theoretical. It was observable, repeatable, and appearing the same way—again and again. Leaders were doing everything they had been trained to do, yet still experiencing the quiet erosion of clarity, energy, and conviction.

This is the moment where leadership stops being a question of knowledge—and becomes a question of conditioning.

Naming the Pattern:
The Moment of Awakening

Somewhere along the way, often in a quiet moment between demands, a different question begins to surface: Is this exhaustion proof that I'm failing—or proof that I've outgrown the way I've been living? That question marks the beginning of awakening.

Patterns are faithful. They repeat until they are interrupted. The Performance Paradox is, at its core, a pattern: perform to belong, achieve to be valued, prove yourself to stay safe. It persuades you that rest must be earned, that your worth is negotiable, that your identity is flexible as long as the metrics look good. For years, perhaps decades, this pattern may have kept you afloat. But the season you are entering now requires more from you than survival. It requires a new pattern formation to become someone who can lead under pressure without abandoning yourself in the process.

To move toward that kind of leadership, you must first be willing to see the pattern in your own life. Maybe it began when a parent's approval seemed to hinge on your performance. Maybe it deepened when you learned that teachers noticed you more when you overprepared. Maybe it took root when your first manager pulled you aside and said, "I know I can always count on you," and something in you translated that praise as a binding contract. Maybe it solidified the first time you were "the only one" in a room and decided, consciously or not, that the safest thing to be was palatable.

However it formed, the internal message often sounds the same: If I do more, I will be more. If I slow down, I will fall behind. If I rest, something will break, and it might be me. When identity is outsourced to performance, the gap between who you are and who you pretend to be gradually widens. That gap is where resentment grows. It is where anxiety multiplies. It is where fatigue masquerades as duty. Left unnamed, that gap eventually becomes a chasm. Naming the pattern is the beginning of reclaiming agency.

So I will ask you, as if we were sitting across from each other: Where in your life have you been performing for approval rather than leading from identity? Whose opinion quietly dictates your sense of worth? What role have you outgrown but continue to inhabit because you are afraid of what might happen if you step out of it? Where are you holding everything together because you believe, often without saying it out loud, that if you let go, everything—and everyone—will fall apart?

These questions are not meant to shame you. They are meant to free you from a story that has run long enough. You cannot outperform a misaligned identity. You can only exhaust yourself trying. Pattern recognition is the first act of courage. Challenging it is the second. Pattern creation is the work that will carry you into Athleadership.

Why This Is Not a Breakdown: The Beginning of Becoming

If, as you read, something in you has been nodding quietly—if you feel seen, unsettled, maybe even a little exposed—do not rush past that feeling. What you are experiencing is not evidence that you are falling apart. It is evidence that a deeper part of you is waking up.

We have been conditioned to treat exhaustion as failure, to treat doubt as weakness, and to treat questions about who we are becoming as dangerous. Yet both neuroscience and lived wisdom tell another story. The brain rewires most powerfully in moments of friction and dissonance, when old pathways begin to loosen, and new ones begin to take hold.[15] The soul grows most honestly when the masks that once kept us safe no longer fit.

What feels like breaking is often the beginning of becoming.

As a high performer just like you, I have lived this on both sides of the table. I've worked inside a company, and I've run my own. In both environments, the demands on leaders were relentless. Without a new way to lead from within, the cost for me was my health, my sleep, and a misplaced identity—until I made a conscious decision to pivot, to create a new operating model that could hold both success and fulfillment.

I had to learn, sometimes the hard way, that you can't build a sustainable life on a foundation of constant self-betrayal.

For leaders who have spent years performing at a high level, awakening rarely arrives as a dramatic epiphany. It shows up as a longing you can't easily describe, as a discontent that no promotion seems to ease, as an inner tug toward alignment that refuses to be silenced. You notice that the strategies that once made you successful now leave you depleted. You realize the applause you once craved lands hollow. You begin to suspect that the version of you the world celebrates is not the full truth of who you are. This is not collapse. It is calibration.

Moments under pressure feel so destabilizing because they expose the gap between who you have been and who you are called to become. They reveal where your inner architecture needs reinforcing, where old patterns need releasing, where your "why" needs reclaiming. They are not asking you to prove yourself; they are inviting you to meet yourself and look at yourself in a new way. You are not behind. You are not broken. You are being rebuilt.

This threshold—the space between the old script and the new story—is the most fertile ground for transformation. It is the place where Athleadership truly begins, not as a concept but as a lived reality. Athleadership does not ask you to abandon the strength you have built. It asks you to aim it. It does not strip you of ambition. It anchors it. It does not diminish your drive. It aligns it with who you are becoming. You were not born ready. You are built ready.

Purpose is not something you perform. It is something you practice.

Identity is not something you inherit. It is something you condition.

The Performance Paradox is not just a crisis of overwork. It is a crisis of identity. And identity, once reclaimed, becomes the most renewable form of power a leader can possess. When your identity is intact, pressure does not fracture you; it focuses you. When your identity is aligned, change does not erode you; it matures you. When your identity is rooted, performance becomes less about proving your worth and more about expressing who you already are.

The work ahead is not about learning how to do more. It is about learning how to become more yourself under pressure.

3

What's Missing Is Purpose in Practice, Not Just on Paper

"When you're surrounded by people who share a passionate commitment around a common purpose, anything is possible."

—Howard Schultz, Former CEO of Starbucks

I didn't learn about purpose in a boardroom. I learned it standing next to a jammed printer.

In my early twenties, I applied for the same internship at Victoria's Secret *eight* times. *Eight.* Each *no* felt louder than the last, and when the yes finally came, it didn't land me in a boardroom. It landed me in the copy room—refilling toner, stapling press clips, filing packets with names I didn't recognize. No one paid any attention to me or knew who I was.

Outside, I looked driven. Inside, I felt overlooked. While I finally made it and got the job, I believe each *no* had chipped away at my confidence, and it was hard to get it back when I spent my days in copy-room drudgery. The mindlessness of the job eroded my sense of self-worth. My environment was beating my inner world and changing my self-talk. I was at the bottom of the rung. I was an intern, and my job was to gather press clips from magazines and newspapers that featured the Victoria's Secret models.

One afternoon, while in the copy room making an executive PR report for the C-suite, I was going through a tall stack of fashion magazines looking for our press features. I flipped through *Vogue* magazine, and an ad stopped me cold. One line: *"Within me lives a purpose, a reason I'm here . . . one day soon it will say, 'The world needs you. Are you ready?'"*

I wasn't ready. It felt big, inconceivable, but the word *purpose* shook something loose in my mind. Two years earlier, I'd been given a book by Dr. Myles Munroe called *Understanding Your Potential.* The message stuck with me because it spoke to some of the real questions I was pondering: *What is my purpose? What are my unique abilities? Why on earth am I here?* It made me think about the distinctive purpose of my life. I believed God's plan for everyone was intentional. When would mine lead me? I tore the page out of the magazine and tucked it into my bag because I couldn't stand the idea of missing out on my purpose if it were true. That torn page still sits on my desk today.

It marks the day I started conditioning for a purpose. I couldn't yet see that purpose, but I believed I was heading for it.

Your Story

Your copy room might look nothing like mine. Maybe you're achieving at a high level, but something inside still feels disconnected.

Or maybe you're on the other end of the spectrum: You've been striking the ground faithfully, doing the work, showing up again, and you're wondering why the breakthrough hasn't come yet. Perhaps you *did* take the leap—changed careers, started the business, stepped into the calling, and now you're in the messy middle where purpose feels more costly than clear. You believe in the vision, but the weight of sustaining it is starting to wear on you. Or maybe you're in a season where you don't know what purpose looks like at all. You're functioning, producing, showing up, yet longing for a deeper sense of meaning that doesn't seem to match your current reality.

Purpose doesn't always feel inspiring. Sometimes it feels exhausting, delayed, expensive, and even painfully quiet. **Purpose shows up any place you feel overlooked, in the seasons where you're doing everything "right" and still feel behind, in the tension between who you are and who you're becoming.** If you've felt that tug—the deep discontent, the quiet ache, the gap between where you are and where you sense you're meant to be—you're not off-track. You're being awakened. That gap you feel isn't failure. It's alignment asking for your attention.

Purpose isn't a privilege for a select few. Everyone has a calling, but it rarely shows up with clarity or convenience. Instead, it emerges where you feel stretched, unseen, uncertain, or unfinished. Purpose doesn't strike like a lightning bolt. It's a compass you build, strengthen, and return to, especially when everything else feels uncertain.

When It Stops Working

Thirty-two-year-old Kevin was taught that if he kept doing the same thing, he'd see results. When Kevin was trained as a sales leader, he was taught 10-3-1: for every ten outreaches you make, you'll get three meetings that will lead to one customer. And there may have been a day when this worked like clockwork. But when the market shifted like it has for many leaders, that model stopped working for Kevin. Revenue declined, morale dipped, and the structure he'd always relied on began to wobble. What did Kevin do? He reached for the only thing he still felt he could control.

Kevin had played both soccer *and* baseball in college. His athletic wiring told him what to do when something felt off: increase the reps. But when reps no longer worked for his sales position, Kevin clung to his training. And while business continued to decline, he went to the one arena where reps did still work today: golf. He hit the course obsessively. Not because he loved the game, but because the mechanics of a good swing gave him something he desperately craved: a predictable outcome. Meanwhile, the yard at home began to get a little overgrown, and paperwork at the office began to slide.

Kevin told himself he was showing up at the course every Saturday morning to play with clients, but what was happening in him was deeper than nurturing relationships. Golf wasn't networking; it was numbing. On the course, he could still feel competent even though everything that mattered felt unstable. But perfecting his swing could not save what mattered most: his family, his well-being, or his business.

Kevin didn't need more reps. He needed deeper work.

The better you perform, the more invisible your pressure becomes because people stop checking in on you as a person and only check for the results. High performers don't get asked, "Are you okay?" They get asked, "Can you take this on?"

When Output Replaces Identity

Millions of people face challenges like Kevin. His performance was impeccable, but his nervous system was on the brink. On the outside, he was an organized top performer. He had a title that turned heads, a calendar booked months in advance, frequent-flyer miles, bonuses, and back-to-back accolades. But inside, he was crumbling, inch by inch. He couldn't trace the exact moment his passion turned into pressure, but the symptoms were clear: tight chest, strained sleep, unexplainable exhaustion, and a low-grade anxiety that never fully let go. And here's the twist: Kevin wasn't failing. He was *winning* by every traditional measure of success! However, his wins were no longer tied to his purpose. This is the essence of the Performance Paradox.

Kevin wasn't falling apart because he lacked ability. He was falling apart because no one had ever taught him how to build the inner conditioning required to sustain when pressure hits.

> **We suffer from the Performance Paradox when our wins are no longer tied to our purpose.**

When your drive to succeed outpaces your connection to *why* you started, your purpose goes dormant. This happens slowly. Typically, purpose is at the center of how we begin, helping us get fired up, mission-driven, and full of possibility. But somewhere along the way, we replace purpose with expectations like performance metrics, social status, and salary goals. The praise and applause become addictive, and our purpose can fade into the background. Instead of pursuing a life driven by our deep purpose, we chase shallow accolades that leave us feeling empty. The Performance Paradox occurs when purpose moves from a living conviction to a performative concept. Something you post about but no longer practice. Something you reference but rarely remember. And the more success you earn, the easier it is to lose sight of who you are *within* it. **When performance becomes the platform for your worth, purpose becomes the price you pay.**

That dopamine hit from praise—email shoutouts, likes on LinkedIn, salary bumps—is motivating . . . until it's not. Because when those affirmations become your fuel, you stop checking in with *yourself.* You stop asking the harder questions, like: "Does this align with my values?" "Am I still fulfilled by this work?" "Is the cost of this success one I'm willing to pay?" The world rarely rewards those questions, which creates a feedback loop that keeps our focus on output because that is what others prioritize. As a result, high-functioning, high-performing individuals like Kevin keep sprinting on a treadmill that never stops—until their health, relationships, or sense of self demand an intervention.

And what about our workplaces? Many companies proudly display their mission and vision statements in their lobbies. But how many leaders can *recite* them, let alone *embody* them? Purpose is preached in the brand—but buried in the behavior. This is how the Paradox becomes systemic. Organizations hire those deemed "fit" and reward burnout. Some organizations claim to care about people but pressure those same people to act like machines. It's not surprising that Gallup found only 21–23 percent of global employees are engaged at work, with burnout being a leading cause of turnover and disengagement.[16] Purpose cannot survive where people are taught to perform but not feel.

Let's make it even more personal. Have you ever:

- Stayed silent in a meeting because the risk of speaking up felt higher than the truth?
- Delivered results even while the strategy felt wrong because challenging it felt unsafe?
- Said yes to an opportunity that looked impressive but cost you a piece of yourself?

And if you're reading this thinking, *But I'm not Kevin; I'm not even winning,* hear me out. The Performance Paradox doesn't just affect people who seem or feel accomplished. It affects the discouraged, the stalled, the overlooked, and the exhausted. You can lose yourself long before you ever "make it." Over time, you build a career not on what matters most to you, but on what is most acceptable to others. It doesn't matter whether you've achieved success by sacrificing your purpose or haven't succeeded despite giving it everything you have. The disconnect between your purpose and your output is the root of the exhaustion and weariness beneath the wins. And if you're not careful, you don't just burn out. You burn *away* from the core of who you are.

Every action says: "This is who I am. This is what I stand for. This is how I lead—even when it's hard." That kind of purpose must be *protected*. And that starts with naming it, claiming it, and aligning your performance to it—not the other way around. Because without purpose in practice, performance is unsustainable. You'll keep climbing, but feel emptier with every promotion or new client win. You'll hit goals, but feel disconnected from your own greatness.

Kevin's wake-up call came through panic attacks and a prescription pad. But for many, it manifests in quieter forms: creative fatigue, emotional numbness, and a sudden indifference to work that once brought joy. If something inside you feels exposed—you're realizing that success without self is hollow. A résumé isn't the same as a legacy.

You may be exhausted because you've been strong for too long in a system that doesn't know how to reward authenticity. But here's the invitation to opt out of the system and step into Athleadership, where identity is *who you are at your core*, and purpose is *why you're here*. When those two are disconnected, performance becomes survival. When they are aligned, performance becomes strength. Athleadership is the work of bringing those two back together—you're not led by pressure but built by purpose.

Why We Chase Proving Moments: Neuroscience in Action

Let's talk about what's really happening inside—because the patterns we normalize are not neutral. They are wired into our biology. And until we understand how the brain responds to pressure and proving, we'll continue to mislabel burnout as weakness and high functioning as wellness. What's going on beneath the surface?

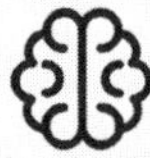 The human brain is wired for two core things: survival and significance. We seek safety and meaning (purpose). But in a world that confuses meaning with metrics, people build systems that reward productivity while quietly starving purpose. Here is what that looks like in the body: Every time you're praised, applauded, rewarded, or validated, your brain releases dopamine, the pleasure chemical that reinforces behavior.[17] This hit of dopamine feels good. It tells your brain: "Do more of that." The presentation that got a standing ovation? Dopamine. The LinkedIn post that racked up 800 likes? Dopamine. It's not vanity. It's neurology.

But a trap forms over time as your brain becomes conditioned to chase the hit. You don't just perform for impact, so you start performing for recognition. Validation becomes fuel. And like any dopamine loop, it requires more to feel the same reward. What once felt exhilarating now feels expected. You raise the bar not because you're growing, but because you're afraid of being irrelevant if you don't. When is it ever enough?

Enter the second chemical: cortisol, the body's primary stress hormone. Cortisol is helpful in short bursts because it gets us moving, sharpens focus, and helps us respond to danger. But when your work-life integration doesn't include any true recovery, cortisol doesn't cycle out. It accumulates. Your body begins to live in a state of chronic activation. I recall going to the doctor to get my hormones checked, as my body was giving signs, but I was not listening. She looked at my results and said: Your cortisol is high at 7:00 a.m. and remains constant through the entire day and evening. That's not normal. That's survival mode. Cortisol ideally has a slow rise in the morning and fluctuates throughout the day. Mine didn't, and the constant level was triggering alarms in my body. My nervous system was locked *on*, which accelerated an autoimmune condition I didn't know I had.

Chronic cortisol disrupts memory, decision-making, immunity, emotional regulation, and sleep. Prolonged exposure to stress can shrink the hippocampus, the area responsible for learning and memory.[18] The very thing you're relying on to lead—your clarity, your cognition, your emotional regulation—is being depleted by the very pressure to perform.

Here's what this looks like in action:

- You do something great.
- You get applause.
- Dopamine fires. You feel alive.
- Next time, you work harder.
- You win again.
- The praise is less. You still crave the high.
- You push more. Cortisol builds.
- You're tired, but can't slow down.
- You're restless even when you "rest."

You start forgetting why you began. Now, it's not joy. It's just a habit.

This isn't alignment, but addiction. You're not addicted to work, exactly, but to the relief that high performance brings. This loop becomes your identity. You're not just working. You're wired to believe that output equals worth. That doing more means being more. And that if you stop—even for a second—you'll fall behind, be forgotten, lose your edge. It's why people like Kevin—people like you and me—we don't crash because we're careless. We crash because we were never taught how to recover. We were rewarded for grit, not roundedness. We were promoted for resilience, not restoration. Trained to "power through," not "pause wisely." We've built systems that reward depletion and mistake burnout for dedication.

If you're reading this thinking, "I *love* what I do," I get it. Purpose-driven people without guardrails are often the most vulnerable to depletion. Passion masks symptoms, mission overrides warning signs, and vision quiets the internal alarms. You justify the cost by the outcome. This is why elite athletes who never learn to rest wisely end up playing through pain until their bodies break. Leaders do the same thing emotionally and psychologically, and our injuries are harder to detect and diagnose. Purpose-driven leaders are those who put personal and professional meaning at the center of their work. It is a powerful success indicator that has an outcome not only for the leader but also for the organization.

What Happens When Purpose Turns into Pressure?

Humans were not created for constant output; we were created for oscillating between natural cycles of performance and recovery. For most of us, we do best with 90–120-minute cycles of energy, focus, and brain function, then the body signals for rest. Neuroscience calls these ultradian rhythms. When you override those signals again, your brain normalizes depletion. You lose the ability to sense your own feelings. This is what it looks like:

- You're answering emails while making dinner.
- You're listening to your child talk while scanning tomorrow's calendar.
- You're in a meeting but thinking about a deadline.

- You finish a project but can't celebrate because you're already behind on the next task.
- Your mind never fully shuts off, because the pressure never fully lets up.

You become a human toggle switch—on for everyone, off for no one—and your purpose becomes the very thing draining you. This is why healthy performance requires boundaries, recovery, and emotional detachment. This is what it sounds like:

- "I've done enough for today."
- "My worth doesn't rise or fall with productivity."
- "Rest is not a reward—it's a requirement."

It also means cultivating a healthy detachment. This isn't apathy. This is an agency. Detachment means you can care deeply without being consumed. It means your self-worth isn't on the line every time you say no. You don't have to answer every question or respond to every email. It means you *own your work*, but it doesn't own you. This is where the *real* performance revolution begins. When we pause intentionally, we optimize instead of falling behind. Neuroscience supports this. After periods of rest, the prefrontal cortex—the part of the brain responsible for strategy, creativity, and focus—functions best.[19] When you step away, ideas incubate and clarity sharpens. While you sleep, your brain undergoes detoxification. Recovery is necessary for success.

Your biology and brilliance can become a form of bondage. Athleadership acknowledges this and doesn't treat high performers like problems to fix, but leaders to realign. It understands that performance and purpose must be copilots. Sustainable excellence isn't just a systems upgrade, but it's a nervous system upgrade. You can rewire how you lead. But first, you must know what you're wired for, and part of that is living a purposeful life.

Purpose Is a System

Leadership is the number one creator of value in any organization. It's at risk because too many talented people are moving fast without a compass. When speed outruns direction, performance wavers, teams become fragile, and good leaders start to feel like impostors in their own careers.

We've been sold a hollow version of purpose, but it cannot be captured in a single sentence that can be repeated on a slide for the town hall or a LinkedIn post. Purpose is simply the reason a person, organization, or entity exists. It describes the ultimate intent of their impact on the world. It is not simply words on paper. In practice, it guides how you aim your energy when the week tilts, how you filter choices when everything looks urgent, and how you return to center when pressure rises. It is a powerful decision anchor to define what you will or won't do and why.

People make numerous daily decisions (some estimate as much as 35,000 a day), ranging from trivial to meaningful, and this cumulative choice burden can contribute to decision fatigue.[20] Purpose in practice becomes a decision-making filter when the lines blur between what is important, urgent, and distracting. We lose our accuracy and edge, which causes us to waste precious time. Your purpose should anchor why you are here, and if you don't use it as a compass, you will wind up someplace you don't belong. But used properly, your purpose can accelerate your success. Let's look at two examples. First, Jesus Christ allowed his purpose to lead him, and he changed the world in three public years. Isaac Newton who at only 25 years old had made some of the most significant breakthroughs in what would become modern science. They didn't have endless time, but they were anchored in purpose and intention, which allowed their work to have an impact long after their earthly lives.

Purpose Is a Brain-Based Advantage

Many people mistake their talents or experiences for their purpose, but your talents are tools you use, and your job is a vehicle driven. Your purpose is the compass that guides you to meaning and the mark you leave on the world. Despite this, according to *Harvard Business Review*, fewer than 20 percent of leaders have clearly identified their purpose—and even fewer have written it down.[21] That means most of us are leading lives, teams, and organizations without a conscious compass. Purpose is the throughline beneath every season, role, reinvention, and everyday action, and pursuing it rewires your brain to think about more than simple achievement.

The key to truly harnessing your purpose is conditioning. That comes from returning to it as you make your decisions, building your relationships and aligning your priorities around it. Tapping into this fuels transformative performance. It's about doing the right things—on purpose, with purpose, for purpose—instead of just doing more and more and more.

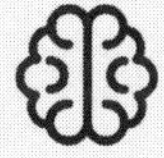

The brain is wired for a purpose, and following it activates neural regions associated with motivation, reward, and resilience. You literally become more focused, more energized, and more likely to persevere through difficulty. Purpose isn't soft—it's strategic. Research shows that having a sense of purpose is also associated with lower levels of cortisol (the primary stress hormone), improved immune function, and even increased longevity.[22]

Purpose helps the brain filter what matters. It quiets the noise. It aligns your attention and energy. In a world of distractions, that is a competitive edge. That's how leaders become forces of change.

When purpose is conditioned, your identity (who you are) and your assignment (why you're here) start working together. When this happens, performance stops being a way to prove you belong and becomes a way to express who you are. That's the work of Athleadership.

In the next chapter, we move from *understanding* purpose to *engineering* it into your leadership, using the same principles we see in elite athletes: intentional reps, clear foundation, measurable growth, and a game plan you can run. You're not here to outrun burnout, but to build a life—and a legacy—on purpose.

PART II

The Athleadership System

Conditioning Leaders to Perform When It Counts

4

Introducing Athleadership

"Performance depends on the brain's ability to regulate stress and remain adaptive in the face of uncertainty."

—Dr. Hayley North, Neuroscientist

There comes a moment in every leader's life when the noise quiets just long enough for you to hear a truth you've been outrunning. It's usually a whisper that cuts deeper than any shout: *You're no longer leading from who you are. You're leading from who you've become.* Most leaders don't talk about this moment, but every leader has lived it. It starts as a slow drift away from yourself. Then, there's a subtle compromise of identity. When your responsibilities multiply faster than your inner resources, your purpose and identity begin to erode, but it can be hard to notice because success along the way can build a beautiful cage—one lined with accomplishment, admiration, and expectations that harden into obligations.

Identity and purpose don't vanish in a single moment. They dim as they get buried beneath the growing weight of who your work requires

49

you to be. Then, one day, you recognize that you have strayed far from your purpose. For me, it was a question that I could no longer swallow: "When did you stop being you?" I didn't have an answer, but I had a memory of what it felt like to be a version of myself I had long forgotten. And in that moment, my mind went back—not to a boardroom, not to a breakthrough, not to a win—but to a track. I remembered the rubber beneath my feet and the air that brimmed with possibility. I heard my breath echoing in my chest like a promise: *You were built to rise.* The track was my home base, where my mind, my body, and my purpose aligned without effort. I didn't have language to describe what I was learning, but now I can put it into words. Identity is not something you discover once. It's something you return to again and again.

Years later, after building a business, a brand, a reputation, and a life that looked steady from the outside, I found myself back on that track but because my life and well-being demanded it. I was haunted by the grief of dreams I hadn't allowed myself to mourn, and the slow unraveling that happens when you spend too long being everything to everyone and nothing to yourself.

As life becomes more complicated, as success becomes something you pursue as a given, it becomes harder to navigate change in a way that honors you as a whole person. But when your purpose is your compass, you can stay true to yourself, even when everything and everyone around you pulls in opposite directions.

As expectations, obligations, and responsibilities mount, we keep performing, but true leadership demands something deeper. It demands identity, which the world cannot give you or take from you, as long as you follow your purpose. Your identity will grow with you. It is the person you are becoming, but it doesn't lose sight of who you are.

That day, standing on the track, I reclaimed the mindset that had shaped me long before adulthood complicated my clarity. I was an athlete: conditioned to rise, built to push through discomfort, able to breathe when the world accelerates, able to face pressure without losing myself. I was someone who refused to shrink. That was the moment Athleadership began, not as a business, not as a curriculum, not as a framework, but as a quiet revelation: *You don't grow out of being an Athleader. You return to it. And when you do, everything changes.* The game around you—the deadlines, the demands, the pivots, the scrutiny—is not where performance is born. Performance is born within you.

Why Leadership Now Requires an Athlete's Mindset

The pace of change, the compression of timelines, the nonstop urgency threaded through modern work—none of it resembles the environment our biology evolved for. The human brain is now experiencing more cognitive load in a single week than previous generations experienced in months.

This pace of change makes it more difficult to concentrate as rapid decisions pile up. Instead of flow, we often exist in a state of relentless mental churn that hums beneath even our best days. But, eventually, it surfaces and we can't pretend that everything is fine.[23] A global Deloitte study found that overwhelm is now the default operating state for more than half of all workers. Burnout has escalated so sharply that the World Health Organization officially classified it as an "occupational phenomenon."[24] But behind those headlines and statistics sits a deeper, more personal truth we rarely admit out loud: Our nervous systems were not built for this level of sustained pressure.

The people who thrive don't necessarily have the fanciest résumés, most impressive strategies, or the appearance of confidence. They aren't the people who avoid uncertainty, which is becoming nearly impossible. Instead, the people who rise when volatility spikes—the ones who stay sharp, grounded, and centered when chaos descends and intensity ramps up—share one common denominator: elite athletic mental conditioning. Elite athletes are built for the very pressure the rest of the world is drowning in. They don't collapse when the moment intensifies—they calibrate. They don't fracture under scrutiny—they narrow their focus. They don't lose themselves when the noise rises—they sink deeper into identity. The reason for this has nothing to do with physical talent and everything to do with mental architecture.

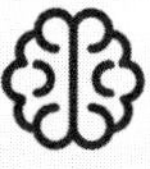 Dr. Michael Mannino—neuroscientist, cofounder of Syneurgy AI, and chief science officer at Flow Research Collective—describes it this way: An elite athlete's neural architecture literally adapts over time to meet the demands of volatility.[25]

Years of purposeful stress exposure, repetition, micro-recovery, and feedback loops don't just build muscle—they rewire the brain. Athletes create structural changes that allow them to process information faster, regulate emotion under pressure, reset quickly after mistakes, recover after emotional strain, and make instinctive yet sound decisions when the stakes are highest. Leaders today are being asked to navigate the same cognitive, emotional, and psychological intensity as elite athletes—but they lack the conditioning. While athletes prepare for pressure long before the pressure arrives, leaders are expected to endure pressure they never prepared for. While athletes rehearse the moment before the moment, leaders are expected to figure it out while the moment unfolds. While athletes build an identity sturdy enough to hold when everything external shifts, leaders are expected to lead others even when they can't recognize themselves.

The quiet crisis beneath the burnout epidemic is a crisis of capacity. This is why so many brilliant, capable, experienced, deeply committed leaders feel stretched thin, scattered, fatigued, or ashamed that their best thinking isn't showing up when it matters. This happens because the game has changed, but their internal arena has not been conditioned to match it.

Elite athletes have a set of transferable qualities that map directly onto the demands of leadership today:

- Discipline that shows up even when motivation doesn't
- Resilience that rebounds instead of resets the whole system
- Team collaboration that becomes instinctive rather than forced
- Strategic focus sharpened through years of pressure, repetition, and correction
- Identity clarity that remains intact even when outcomes shift

These are not personality traits, but conditioned capacities. Athletes can rewire their internal systems through intentional conditioning—physical, mental, emotional, and neurological. And here is the revelation that changed my work forever: You do not need to be an athlete to develop an athlete's mind; you only need their conditioning method, which

- Conditions your nervous system, not just your skills
- Strengthens your identity, not just your productivity
- Rewires your patterns, not just your plans
- Protects your capacity as fiercely as you protect your performance

Unlike athletic conditioning, leadership development has failed leaders because it never taught them how to carry the pressure of leading. Traditional leadership models prepare you for everything *around* you—strategy, communication, influence, decision-making—but almost nothing *within* you. And yet, it is your internal arena that determines whether you rise, fracture, or plateau. That's why this era of accelerated pressure and unprecedented complexity requires an entirely new discipline that is grounded in neuroscience, shaped by elite performance, and built around identity, resilience, agility, and sustainable capacity. An effective conditioning method does more than elevate leaders—it fortifies them.

Athleadership is a system of mental conditioning that strengthens the arena within so that leaders can withstand, adapt, and rise in the game around them. At its heart, leadership is entwined with identity, alignment, and conditioning. It is not about performance, but about becoming.

Athleadership is a system of mental conditioning that strengthens the arena within so that leaders can withstand, adapt, and rise in the game around them.

The Arena Within: What Elite Athletes Know That Leaders Must Learn

The first time I understood the true meaning of the arena, it wasn't sitting in a classroom or observing a boardroom. It was standing beside a world-renowned athlete in one of the most pressurized moments of his career and watching him choose identity over circumstance. His name is Oguchi "Guch" Onyewu, and long before I understood Athleadership as a discipline, he showed me what it looked like.

I worked with him during the lead-up to the 2010 World Cup, a moment that should have been triumphant, defining the kind of chapter athletes dream of from the time they kick their first ball. But his story, at that precise moment, was one of resilience. He was returning from a devastating injury. His body had healed, but his future was still in question. And layered on top of the physical recovery was the weight of something even heavier: a wave of racist hostility and public scrutiny that would have shattered most people's sense of self. In 2009, he was taunted with racial slurs by an opponent during a Belgian league playoff game.

When I watched him walk into that moment, he wasn't clinging to a jersey or a title or the admiration of crowds. He was anchored in something deeper, an inner resolve that didn't rise and fall with opinion or outcome. His identity was bigger than the game unfolding around him. This was my intimate window into the arena, not the stadium filled with fans, but the internal space where pressure collides with purpose, where doubt meets discipline, where fear either fractures you or forges you.

What struck me most was not Guch's physical strength, but the quiet precision of his mental response. He did not perform on adrenaline but through his identity. And when I asked him how he kept his center through the chaos, he said something I will never forget: "If you fear failure, you also fear success. They're hand in hand. I pride myself on being comfortable in uncomfortable situations." That wasn't bravado. That was conditioning.

Behind the public wins and losses were years of neural hardwiring shaped by adversity, repetition, and recalibration. Years of falling and rising. Years of learning to master the mind long before mastering the moment. Years of becoming adaptable enough to thrive across eight countries, multiple languages, and more transitions than most leaders will ever face. Guch's inner arena, which he cultivated quietly, deliberately, relentlessly, later carried him into leadership roles far beyond sport, including secretary general for Royal Excelsior Virton in Belgium, CEO and founder of ONYX Elite, and vice president of sporting for the US Soccer Federation. He didn't get there because he played at the highest level, but because he had conditioned himself to think, recover, and respond at the highest level. Guch was the first proof of something I would go on to see in thousands of Athleaders across industries, ages, and backgrounds: Your external game can only be as strong as your internal arena.

Elite athletes cultivate their inner arena before they ever play the game. They learn how to regulate their breath under exhaustion, adapt strategy when conditions shift, stay grounded when the crowd roars or goes silent, and reset their mind after failure. They also learn how to carry purpose when pressure tries to break their confidence. But athletes don't have stronger minds than other people. They just have stronger conditioning.

Neuroscience confirms what performance has always revealed: Athletes' brains reorganize under repeated stress exposure, reflection, and recovery. Their neural pathways strengthen and automatically improve, their fear response softens, and their resilience accelerates. They prepare for pressure long before they experience it.[26]

Years after my work with Guch, I began studying what separated leaders who rose under pressure from those who unraveled. At first, the patterns felt anecdotal, even coincidental: Why did so many of the best leaders I coached have athletic backgrounds? Why did they adapt more quickly, recover more steadily, and lead more courageously? What made their presence different? Their resilience different? Their mindset different? The answer: Their wiring was different because they had spent years conditioning their internal arena.

The statistics only confirmed what experience had already suggested: Former athletes, particularly women, are strongly represented in executive leadership roles. An EY/espnW study found that 94 percent of women in the C-suite had participated in sports, with 80 percent of Fortune 500 female executives reporting athletic backgrounds.[27] While equivalent population-level statistics are not available for executives overall, institutional leadership analyses suggest that athletic experience is common across senior leaders more broadly.[28] This pattern is commonly attributed not to chance, but to the performance mindset developed through sport. The qualities the world now demands of leaders—agility through change, resilience under pressure, alignment in complexity, well-being that sustains performance—are the very qualities athletes spend years cultivating before they ever enter a spotlight. As I witnessed these patterns, first with athletes, then with executives, Athleadership began to take shape. Not as a metaphor or a catchy phrase, but as a system that supported a way of thinking and being. What elite athletes know and leaders must learn is that the game happens around you, but the arena happens within you. Performance is born in the arena.

The System: The Playbook for Becoming

Athleadership is not the next evolution of leadership theory; it's a new discipline for those committed to becoming the leader the moment demands. The world needs leaders who go beyond simple mastery of competencies and can master their capacity. Leaders whose nervous systems are built for the speed, strain, and scrutiny of modern work. When the people around you start to unravel, when the pressure mounts, and when demands feel inhuman, well-conditioned leaders can stand steady and think clearly. Athleadership can help us get there.

The Athleadership System

Every movement has a moment when its structure becomes undeniable. I introduced the four pillars in the preface, but I'll repeat them here:

1. The MVP Foundation
2. The Core 4
3. The Conditioning Process
4. The 90-Day Way

This is the internal progression every leader must move through to perform under pressure without losing themselves in the process.

Athleadership: The Definition

Athleadership is the performance operating system for modern leadership—built on the elite athletic mindset and designed to condition the mental and neurological capacities leaders rely on to perform under pressure, adapt through accelerating change, and stay anchored to purpose. Grounded in neuroscience and proven in elite sport, it equips leaders to perform when it counts. Simply put, Athleadership demonstrates that leaders aren't born—they're built. And they're built through conditioning. Athleadership provides an operating system that empowers you to utilize your compass to navigate uncertainty and stay anchored. Through the Core 4, you can build the mental muscles to accelerate forward with the conditioning reps to become. All while building the 90-day plan that will take you through life season by season.

Athleadership is proven, tested, and trusted by leaders worldwide who have conditioned themselves to lead when it counts.

Simply put: Athleadership demonstrates that leaders aren't born— they're built.

The Four Pillars of Athleadership

Now we turn toward the heart of the work—the part of the system that begins rewiring your internal world so you can rise in your external one.

Each pillar is written not as a list, but as lived experience.

 ## 1. The MVP Foundation— Identity: Your Compass in Chaos

When pressure hits, the brain does not search for strategy, but for something solid enough to stand on. That something is identity, which is defined by your mission, vision, and purpose (MVP). These three anchors form the foundation the brain relies on to stay grounded under strain.

Neuroscience shows that when your identity is clear, the prefrontal cortex, which is responsible for decision-making, emotional regulation, and strategic thinking, stays online longer than stress. But when identity is unclear, the brain is reactive, emotional regulation is weak, creativity shuts down, and fear shapes behavior. When leaders with extraordinary skill and experience are not anchored in their identity—their MVP— they can unravel in moments of uncertainty.

 ## 2. The Core 4—The Mental Engine That Expands Capacity

The Core 4 are neuroscience-backed mental capacities that determine how your mind performs when life applies pressure. They are shaped through neuroplasticity, the brain's ability to rewire itself through repetition, regulation, and reflection. Each one governs a different part of your adaptive architecture—the internal scaffolding that allows you to lead under change, uncertainty, and intensity. Together, they form your mental engine rooted in neuroscience and performance psychology.

⟳ Agility

Agility is your ability to stay clear, steady, and strategic when the world refuses to cooperate with your plans. It's about finding stability and staying grounded, thinking clearly, and adapting through change without losing yourself. Neuroscience calls it *cognitive flexibility*—the capacity to shift mental sets, update strategy, and make decisions in ambiguity. Psychology calls it *emotional agility*—staying grounded enough to respond instead of reacting. It is how athletes pivot on instinct, and how leaders must pivot under pressure.

◌ Resilience

Resilience is the ability to rise through pressure. It is the internal elasticity to recover, rebuild, and become stronger in the places life stretches you most. Resilience is not bouncing back to who you were; it's growing forward into who you're becoming, without losing yourself in the process. Resilience is the brain's recovery capacity, the speed at which you return to clarity after disruption, disappointment, conflict, or adversity. It is your ability to metabolize stress instead of absorbing it.

In athletes, resilience shows up as a rapid reset. In leaders, it shows up as emotional recovery that keeps your identity from collapsing under pressure.

▷⋮◁ Alignment

Alignment is purpose in motion, the ongoing discipline of coming back to what matters, recalibrating your choices to your core truth, and moving in the direction of your life, leadership, and calling keep pointing you toward, even when the world pulls you off center. It is what neuroscientists call *neural coherence*, which is when what you say, choose, prioritize, and embody are no longer at war.

When alignment strengthens,

- Decision-making becomes cleaner.
- Boundaries become clearer.
- Confidence becomes steadier.
- Energy stops leaking into the wrong places.

Alignment is purpose, lived.

✿ Well-Being

Well-being is the foundation of sustainable strength that makes high performance repeatable. It encompasses physical readiness, mental recovery and reset, behavioral boundaries and focus.

Most of us don't burn out because we lack skill. We burn out because we are either operating outside of our strengths (MVP) or because we have not mastered the oscillation of performance and recovery. Our well-being must be central to our operating system to sustain performance. It requires our physical readiness, mental recovery, and reset, as well as the healthy maintenance of boundaries.

The Core 4 gives you the internal bandwidth to meet life at full intensity without collapsing beneath it.

 ## 3. The Conditioning Process— The Becoming

Understanding the Core 4 does not change you, but conditioning does. Conditioning is the method that rewires your mental patterns and nervous system so that pressure no longer pulls you out of alignment. It propels you forward, no matter the change or the uncertainty.

It includes four core elements:

1. **DRILLS—Neuroscience-backed micro skill-building techniques:** A drill is a *micro-tool*—a short, repeatable action that interrupts your stress response and reengages your ability to think clearly under pressure. It is the mental equivalent of an athlete practicing footwork, free throws, or starts out of the blocks.

2. **REPS—Identity builders:** Repeated actions that strengthen who you are becoming. (Example: A 60-second centering rep. Pause for 60 seconds. Do not speak. Do not respond. Do not rush.) Reps are not tasks; they are signals to your nervous system. Every rep wires the identity you intend to inhabit.

3. **RHYTHM—Urgency interrupter:** Rhythm protects your mind from the chaos of constant demand. It creates predictable pacing —morning resets, weekly alignment, monthly reflection—that stabilizes your internal world even when your external world is unpredictable. Rhythm is what keeps you human in environments that reward burnout.

4. **RECOVERY—Capacity restorer:** Recovery is not withdrawal. It is recalibration. It is the process that restores your nervous system so you can meet tomorrow with clarity rather than exhaustion. Recovery expands your capacity more than effort ever will.

This is the pillar that differentiates Athleadership from other approaches. Simply put, what you do daily determines who you become permanently.

4. The 90-Day Way—Your Season of Transformation

Transformation requires rhythm or recommitment over time. This is why athletes prepare in seasons. The human brain is built for defined cycles of focus, integration, and recovery. This is the method that makes change stick.

The 90-Day Way gives you the season you need to become who you are meant to be next. At my company, Velvet Suite, we run our entire business by the 90-Day Way. It allows each of our A-team to set personal and professional goals against their MVP and their professional growth opportunities. We look at each quarter as a time to pursue those priorities, grow, learn, and achieve. At the end of each quarter, we then take a half-day reset to reflect, recharge, and recommit to our next 90-day season. We call this season by season approach our foundation for forever.

The System in One Sentence

If you remember only one line from this chapter, let it be this: Athleadership is the modern operating system that builds the leader you are becoming—from the inside out—through identity, mental conditioning, and rhythmic transformation.

The Becoming in Real Life

The following examples offer glimpses of how the four Athleadership pillars can flex to meet different needs.

The Executive Who Couldn't Breathe Anymore

Sandra was brilliant, strategic, trusted, respected—and exhausted in a way she couldn't fully articulate. Her days were a blur of meetings, decisions, crises, expectations, and urgency.

She kept pushing—because that's what leaders do—until one day the pressure stopped being an external force and became an internal weight. Sandra's words to me were simple: "I'm tired of being the person everyone counts on while feeling like I'm losing myself."

She needed her compass back, so we rebuilt her MVP Foundation. Sandra's mission clarified her contribution, her vision restored her direction, and her purpose reconnected her to meaning. And she said something I will never forget: "It's the first time in years I've felt like I was leading from myself, not from the expectations around me." That is Athleadership: Identity before performance. Compass before capacity. Being before doing. Sandra became an Athleader.

The Senior Leader Stuck in Reaction Mode

Victor was seasoned, the kind of leader people follow without thinking twice, but change had accelerated faster than his resilience could absorb. He felt constantly behind, pulled, reactive. "I'm always fixing. I'm never leading."

When we assessed his Core 4, the gap was obvious: His agility was high, his alignment was strong—but his resilience had collapsed. Victor wasn't broken; he was unconditioned. So, we built a resilience cadence:

- Micro-recoveries
- Daily decompression
- A 90-second emotional reset
- Weekly rhythm checks
- Boundary reinforcement

Within six weeks, Victor became an Athleader and said, "I didn't change my circumstances. I changed my capacity." That is what it means to be an Athleader.

The Leader Who Felt Out of Position in Her Own Life

On paper, Raha had everything: the title, team, influence, credibility. But her days no longer matched her values, her calendar no longer matched her purpose, and her decisions no longer matched her identity. She said, "It feels like I've succeeded my way into misalignment."

We redefined alignment, not as a nice-to-have, but as something the brain needs to function well. Raha learned that when your identity is out of sync, it drains mental energy, and when your values are in conflict, the brain reacts as if under threat.

As Raha's alignment returned, her clarity did, too. Her emotional coherence strengthened and her decision fatigue diminished. "I didn't just get my purpose back. I got myself back." She became an Athleader.

The Call to Becoming

Somewhere in this chapter, you likely felt a flicker of recognition. And now that you've seen the system, you understand the architecture, and recognize the gap, there is only one question left: *Are you willing to become the leader your moment is asking for?* Your becoming begins now.

5

Defining Your MVP—Mission, Vision, and Purpose

"Tap into your purpose. Tap into your passion.
This is your true legacy, we all can make a difference."

—Troy Vincent, Executive Vice President, Football Operations, NFL,
and Walter Payton NFL Man of the Year Award Recipient

At the center of the Athleadership system lies your mission, vision, and purpose—your MVP:

- **Mission:** What you contribute to accomplish the vision
- **Vision:** Where you are going
- **Purpose:** Why you exist

A CEO Who Refused to Win at the Cost of Himself

When I think about a leader who lives his MVP in real time, I think of Jamal Muashsher, president and CEO of Valvoline Global Operations.

On paper, his story looks like a classic ascent—global P&L, major transformation, big expectations—but that's not what makes him an Athleader. It's what he decided to protect while everything around him was accelerating.

When Jamal stepped into the CEO role, he inherited more than a title. He inherited a mandate: lead through a complex transformation, deliver for shareholders, navigate global uncertainty, and do it without breaking the people—or himself—in the process. It would have been easy to default to the usual playbook: work more, sleep less, sacrifice family "for a season," push harder, and hope resilience shows up on command. Instead, he did something most leaders talk about but rarely commit to: He anchored in purpose before he escalated performance.

If you ask Jamal what his company does, he'll talk to you about performance, innovation, and helping customers profitably grow. But if you ask him what *he* is here to do, his answer shifts gears. "My purpose is to enable others to achieve the best possible outcomes," he told me. "And that includes my team. That includes my family. That includes me." Those are not just elegant words. They are decisions. He decided: *I'm going to coach my people, not just manage the numbers.* He decided: *I'm going to be home for my family, not just send them what's left of me.* He decided: *My personal well-being is not negotiable—it's a requirement of my leadership.*

When one of his direct reports was pushing too hard, Jamal didn't celebrate the grind. He pulled them aside and said, "Take care of yourself. Your people, your family needs you to be at your best." That is not a soft sentiment. That is strategy because Jamal knows what neuroscience confirms: A depleted leader can't think clearly, connect deeply, or lead sustainably.

His history is one of transformation—business transformation, yes, but also personal transformation. Again, he has chosen to navigate transition with resilience instead of reactivity. He doesn't pretend the road-blocks don't exist. He expects them. And he trusts that if the purpose is clear, he and his team will find the best path through.

Ask him what he worries about, and he won't say "the market" first. He'll say, "I worry when leaders stop taking care of themselves. Because when you're not at your best, your ability to influence, to decide, to navigate complexity—it all erodes."

In action, MVP has tremendous power:

- **Mission:** Enable others—teams, customers, family— to achieve the best possible outcomes.
- **Vision:** Lead a global enterprise through transformation in a way that leaves people better, not broken.
- **Purpose:** Become the kind of leader who refuses to trade his humanity for his results.

You can see it in Jamal's calendar: time blocked for family (i.e., dinner together and coaching his daughter's sports), not just board meetings. You can see it in his conversations: questions that coach people toward their potential, not just critiques of their performance. You can see it in the way his team describes him: steady, prepared, human.

Jamal's story matters here because it proves something many leaders doubt: You don't have to choose between performance and purpose. You don't have to sacrifice your well-being to be effective. You don't have to abandon your family to lead at the highest level. But you do have to decide who you are going to be—before the pressure spikes. That is the work of MVP.

Purpose Is Oxygen

Leadership doesn't often begin with confidence; it often begins with a crisis. It is why you are called to the table, called up from the bench. Purpose arrives as oxygen.

The moment your plans unravel. The moment your identity feels shaken. The moment you realize the life you've built is no longer big enough for the truth rising inside you.

That's when leadership begins—not the kind printed on business cards, but the kind etched into your character. It starts with a time of self-discovery to ask yourself: What do you define as success on your terms? What is your motivation? What is driving your decisions—is it from a place of approval, competition, proving, wholeness? Take the time to get honest with yourself. If your motivation is not sustainable, do you know what is?

It starts with a time of self-discovery to ask yourself: What do you define as success on your terms? What is your motivation? What is driving your decisions—is it from a place of approval, competition, proving, wholeness?

Stepping into position requires purpose to lead yourself and others for the long haul. I can attest that many organizations have purpose statements and well-being mantras with good intentions to support people and the culture. However, as leaders, until we master our why and align it to our work, people won't see more than words on paper; they won't see the alignment in our behaviors and actions.

Maybe you're standing in that space today. You've done everything "right." You've succeeded on paper, but you feel the pressure mounting. Yet the default is to work harder, not smarter. The first step in building a rock-solid MVP is to listen. Do a check-in on yourself.

This is where the old metrics start to let you down. Where titles, accolades, and status stop satisfying. You begin to feel a subtle but relentless pull toward more, but not the more you once chased. Not more achievement. Not more applause. *More alignment. More impact. More meaning.* You realize you weren't just built to succeed. You were built to lead—with purpose, when it counts.

But the moment you awaken to this truth is also the moment the pressure intensifies. Suddenly, you're no longer leading from the identity you were handed by others; you're leading from a place of chosen truth. And that kind of leadership will always challenge the old systems.

You may feel alone at times, misunderstood, unseen, possibly disconnected, but hear me clearly: You are not behind. You are breaking through.

Whatever words you decide to create will be tested not on paper but in real-life practice. That is when you will know it is real and highly relevant to your leadership as a compass. In Athleadership, we call that compass your mission, vision, and purpose (MVP), and I'll help you craft your own. It's not branding. *It's your anchor and your compass.*

- **Mission:** How will you accomplish the vision? (What will you do day in and day out?)
- **Vision:** Where do you aspire for your personal and professional life to go? (What is the destination?)
- **Purpose:** Why are you here? (What is the original intent and reason for being?)

When you don't have a compass, you end up saying yes to everything and belonging to nothing. When you do have a compass, you stop negotiating with your values. Decisions speed up. Boundaries get kinder and firmer. Feedback stings less because it's not grading your identity. You can pivot without losing yourself because your *why* holds steady while your *how* adjusts.

Before anyone approved your promotion or rejected your proposal— life handed you pressure reps: disappointments you outlasted, opportunities you created, rooms you steadied. That's durable leadership. This chapter is where we write it down—so it can start leading you back.

Let's Do This

We're going to do this simply. I'll sit with you like I'm across the table on a Sunday night. Our goal is to put your MVP into a few honest sentences that resonate with you, not just on paper but in real life. Then we'll stress-test it against the week you live—meetings, kids' schedules, real budgets, real pressure—so your compass doesn't live on a poster; it lives in your calendar.

If you're thinking, *"I've tried purpose statements before,"* I hear you. Most of those were aspirational paragraphs that sounded great and led you nowhere. This one will be different because we will make it *usable*. **It will help you decide what to protect, what to pause, and what to pass.** It will become the first tool you reach for when requests and meetings are more than the time you have in a day.

In sports, the MVP is the most valuable player, the person everyone can trust under pressure. Your MVP is the *same idea for your life*: It's your championship standard. It tells you the focus for how you will invest your time, talent, and energy; it sets your priorities as a decision filter for what is most important now, what is next, and what can come later. The reason this compass is essential is that in a world that is constantly vying for your time and attention, it is incredibly easy to become distracted by the many responsibilities, requests, and demands that come across your plate daily. This is why we have at the core of our model the MVP, which truly becomes the home base that you come back to each day for your life and leadership. It is what empowers you to not only course correct, but to anchor on what matters most for you in your leadership journey and in each season of your life.

When the week tilts, your MVP acts as a compass, "What's the most valuable move *now*?"—and that is how purpose turns into performance you can trust.

Your Job Is a Tool. Not the Goal.

Before you nail down your MVP, let's clear something up: Your job is *not* your purpose. It's the current gym where you're being conditioned. You might be in a season where your title feels too small for your vision—or too big for your current alignment. Either way, the job is just the *gym*. Your purpose is the *training plan*. When you confuse your job with your assignment, you'll chase validation instead of transformation. But when you understand your job is a conduit, not a crown, you can find peace even in the tension.

Carmen led customer service at a national brand. No big title. No platform. Just a Post-it on her monitor pulled from her purpose statement: **"Be the calm in the storm."** When a company-wide outage left millions without service, it shocked everyone except her that she became *manager of the month*. While panic spread, she steadied her team, kept morale high, and became the emotional anchor for an entire department. She wasn't "in charge" on paper. But she was leading because she practiced her purpose every day. When the moment demanded more, she was already conditioned for it. That's what it looks like when purpose is practiced, and your job becomes the gym for your assignment.

MVP: Your Compass

In sports, the MVP makes an impact that can't be ignored. Not just because they put up points, but because they *elevate* the entire team. The term first gained traction in Major League Baseball (the MLB) in the early 1900s and has since come to symbolize unmatched value, influence, and execution under pressure.

We borrow that idea and flip it inward. Your personal MVP forms the foundational layer of the Athleadership Operating System—your internal scoreboard. When the pressure hits or the path feels unclear, your MVP reminds you who you are, why it matters, and how to move.

When I share with audiences that their driving purpose isn't just a *slogan*, but a way of life, many ask me how to find, how to *discern*, the purpose that propels them. You find it through listening to your life. Studying your history, decoding your past. You find it through times of solitude and disconnection to listen. Too often, we speak without even knowing our own voice.

Your First Essential Step

I'm looking at that torn paper I ripped from a magazine years ago and taped above a wobbly desk: "Within me lives a purpose, a reason I'm here. And one day soon it will say to me, 'Hi there. The world needs you. Are you ready?'" Back then, my honest answer was *no*. It wasn't because I didn't want to be ready, but because I was just beginning the journey of understanding my purpose.

Here's what I want you to hear in this moment: I did not build this work from a platform. I built it in the copy room, the hospital waiting room, reps to run a half-marathon, and the mirror at 6:00 a.m. I built it with doubt in one hand and a pen in the other. The torn paper didn't crown me. It called me to a pursuit of discovery of purpose.

The compass didn't make me visible. It made me faithful through my life's journey.

Here is a little glimpse into the first mission statement I wrote and taped on the mirror in my bathroom over 20 years ago. I would say this to myself in the mirror every day (its words are etched in my memory). It was my lifeline. Starting this business, staring at bills, rejection letters, and unanswered emails. I believe that somewhere, someone will believe in my vision and help me move this mission forward. This became my anchor, my compass to navigate the storms of entrepreneurship and the twists and turns of life, then and even today. It still guides me and keeps me grounded: "I will live each day with purpose, divinely designed by God. I will walk with precision and be guided by purpose. I will receive prosperity and favor in every facet of my life. I am a pioneer; I challenge the status quo. . . ." I've always had three personal anchors, which included: faith, family, and fitness. Each of these anchors has driven me through the good and hard times. This is where purpose isn't performative; it is only transformative when it is lived in, worn, and embodied.

That compass—the discipline of returning to my MVP when everything else shook—became the spine of my life and the seed of a movement. It led me to walk away from what looked safe, to start Velvet Suite when no one was handing out guarantees, and to design a way of building leaders that didn't depend on charisma or perfect circumstances. It's how we created the NFL Player Brand University, then took the same conditioning to influence brands globally. The purpose is to shape lives of intention and accelerated impact with real decisions, real boundaries, and real lives reclaimed. And it was the same compass that led me into true love with my husband, Will. The same compass carried me into motherhood, even when the odds were against me. It is the same compass that sits on my desk and anchors how I plan my day and what I prioritize first on my calendar. It's the compass that keeps me grounded when I go to bed at night in who I am without any performance while still breaking new ground—stretching me to become, again and again. All of it traces back to a copy room, a torn page, and the courage to condition this operating model for myself before I ever offered it to anyone else.

And I'm still looking at that torn paper that announces: "Within me lives a purpose, a reason I'm here. And one day soon it will say to me, 'Hi there. The world needs you. Are you ready?'" And I *still* ask, "Am I ready?" The truest answer is the one I want for you: *I'm ready enough to begin again today.*

If you're reading this with your own contradictions humming—successful and empty, strong and exhausted, loved and lonely—please hear me: The point is not to fix your whole life by Friday. The point is to *root* it. Your MVP is not a performance. It's your protection against identity theft. Most of us were never taught how to protect who we are, so we outsource our worth to titles, timelines, and the next email. Your compass brings it back home.

This is where mindset turns into muscle. It's not hype, but conditioning. The world doesn't slow down. The weeks will still tilt. But with a practiced compass, you stop judging yourself for the wobble and start aiming through it. Under stress, your brain will always try to grab the wheel with fear first; that's biology. Your MVP is the hand on your shoulder that says, "Breathe. Remember who you are. Choose from why, not from panic."

I want this to be a permission slip and a charge. Permission to start where you are—broken pieces and all. Charge to move—one sentence, then one step, then one rep. This is how freedom begins: not with elevation or visibility, but with integrity that no one sees but you . . . and the people who feel the difference when you walk into the room.

Let's bring this all the way home and make it yours. If you're ready, grab a pen or your device. If you're not sure you're ready, grab one anyway. "Ready" isn't a feeling. It's a decision you make before the proof shows up. Let's write your compass. Then we'll use it.

Who do I need to become to live the life I was made for?

Let's break it down:

- **M = Mission:** *How* you move—your daily discipline to accomplish the vision. The actions you take, the values you activate, the ways you serve each and every day.
- **V = Vision:** *Where* you aspire to go. The vivid picture of your future that pulls you forward, even when current circumstances don't.
- **P = Purpose:** *Why* you exist. Your unshakable reason for being—the deeper meaning behind your gifts, your grit, and even your journey. It is your power source and what uniquely defines your contribution.

This is your leadership compass.

Together, MVP becomes a framework that turns identity into action, and action into legacy. It's not poetic—it's practical. It helps you answer the quiet questions high performers often wrestle with but rarely voice:

- *Should I take this opportunity—or let it pass?*
- *Is this alignment—or am I just performing again?*
- *What version of me is making this decision right now?*

When you know your MVP, you stop leading from reaction and start leading from rhythm. Take a clean page. At the top, write: My MVP. Then, line by line, use simple, human words.

The MVP Drafting Lab

This is your simple, clear, foundational system for writing your MVP the Athleadership way. This is where clarity becomes language. We move to very practical illustrations to give you a foundation to build upon. Below is the exact process we've taught to CEOs, athletes, executives, educators, founders, and emerging leaders across continents. It works for anyone, at any stage, because it moves you from *intuition* → *words* → *alignment* → *action.*

Step 1—The Drafting Process

No pressure. No polishing. Just the truth. Think of this like chalk on the locker-room board: quick, loose, honest, human. You'll refine later. First, you need raw material.

Take a moment to reflect on your life. Take a sheet of paper or open your device and look at key milestone moments and experiences that helped shape who you are. These can be from accomplishments like graduations to valley situations such as loss, health challenges, or tragedy. The key is to mark each season of your life with the words to describe defining moments over each decade. Then, go back and circle the words, adjectives, and experiences that marked your life. Those words have clues for your MVP. For example, from what I have shared with you, some of the words that have defined my journey have been faith, overcoming, communication, branding, impacting others, influencing through connection, and so on.

The Athleadership way is that leadership is a lifestyle. It is who you are in every aspect of your life at work, at home, and everywhere in between. As you write your MVP, think upon how you reflect your total life picture, not just your profession.

A. Start with Three Simple Questions

Write one free-flowing paragraph for each:

1. **Mission: How do I move daily to accomplish the vision?**
    - What daily actions align with your highest impact?
    - What do you do so well, it looks effortless—even though it took years to master?
    - What am I naturally compelled to do?
    - What actions define the way I serve others?
    - What strengths show up even when I'm not trying?
    - This encompasses your work today in your profession and how you show up to bring your best talent and experience to accomplish your vision. Your mission can evolve with different seasons of your life.

2. **Vision: Where do you aspire for your life and leadership to go?**
    - What future do I feel responsible for creating?
    - What does my best work make possible five or ten years from now?
    - What legacy am I quietly building?
    - Five years from now, what does success *feel* like in your body, home, and legacy?
    - What do you see that energizes you to keep going when the work gets hard?

3. **Purpose: Why does any of this matter to me (what is the greater meaning that reveals why you are here)?**
    - When have you felt most alive, aligned, and undeniable—and what were you *doing* in that moment?
    - What pain, problem, or pattern in the world do you feel personally responsible to change?

- Who becomes stronger, clearer, or more courageous because you showed up—and *how* do you do that?
- What have you always been drawn to—even before someone paid you to do it?
- What, if removed from my life, would make everything else feel less meaningful?

Don't edit. Don't judge. Just write.

B. Underline the Verbs

Because mission is about action, underline the doing words. These verbs will become your mission anchors.

C. Circle the Nouns

Because vision is about destination, circle the people, places, conditions, outcomes. These nouns become your vision picture.

D. Highlight the Emotional Language

Because purpose is about meaning, highlight words that feel:
- Charged
- Tender
- True
- Courageous
- Confronting

Your body will tell you what matters before your brain does.

E. Pull One Sentence from Each Section

Don't overthink. Pull the sentence that feels most *alive*. These become your
- Rough mission line
- Rough vision line
- Rough purpose line

Step 2—Write Your Mission, Vision, and Purpose Lines

Use these definitions to keep it clean and distinct:

MISSION—How you will accomplish the vision (daily work).
What you commit to doing consistently, regardless of how you feel.

Sentence Starter: "I commit to . . . so that . . ."

**VISION—Where you aspire for your life and leadership
to go (in the future).** This is the long-term picture—
personal and professional—that you feel called toward.

Sentence Starter: "The future I am building looks like . . . because . . ."

PURPOSE—Why you are here (your meaning). The deeper reason
behind your gifts, your grit, and your story. Purpose is the power
source. Purpose stabilizes the brain under uncertainty. Purpose gives
the prefrontal cortex something solid to hold when the world shakes.

A sample template example:
"I exist to ________ by ________ so that ________."

Examples:

- "I exist to awaken potential by elevating purpose so that people
  can lead whole and free."
- "I exist to build trust by creating clarity so that teams can move
  boldly together."
- "I exist to develop leaders by investing deeply so that the work
  and the people both win."

You can refine the grammar later. For now, write it honestly.

Step 3—Stress-Test It with Your Real Life

Ask three questions:

1. Does this feel true in my body?
2. Can I live this on a Tuesday?
3. Would I be proud if my family or friends repeated this about me?

If the answer is yes → keep it.

If the answer is no → refine it.

Step 4—Share It with Your Inner Circle

Purpose grows in community. Share your draft with:

- A family member
- A mentor
- A teammate or colleague
- Someone you lead or influence

Ask them:

- "Where do you see this already alive in me?"
- "What feels missing or unclear?"
- "Does this sound like who I truly am becoming?"
- Let their feedback sharpen the edges, not rewrite your essence.

EXAMPLE 1

Mission		
My mission is to lead my family with love, integrity, and resilience—becoming the everyday example others look to when life gets hard.	My mission is to turn competitive drive into collective strength, developing people and systems that win with consistency, resilience, and purpose.	My mission is to model the kind of strength, faith, and discipline that empowers my children to trust themselves, pursue their calling, and stand tall in any arena.

Vision		
My vision is to live and lead with such alignment that my life becomes proof: You can win at work, thrive at home, and stay grounded in purpose—all while lifting others higher.	My vision is to build a legacy of courage, character, and contribution—shaping a world where my children, my team, and everyone I influence learn to lead from within.	My vision is to build a life where my actions speak louder than my ambition—creating a home, career, and legacy others can point to and say, "That's what purpose in motion looks like."
Purpose		
I exist to create clarity and courage in leaders so they can make decisions that matter.	I exist to bring clarity and courage where pressure creates doubt—helping people rise to who they are capable of becoming.	I exist to create alignment in chaos by restoring focus, calm, and conviction—elevating the performance of every space I enter.

EXAMPLE 2

Mission	Vision	Purpose
I build solutions that solve real problems with integrity and creativity.	To create a business ecosystem where innovation and well-being coexist.	I exist to turn ideas into impact so that people's lives are measurably better.

EXAMPLE 3

Mission	Vision	Purpose
I show up with joy, presence, and patience in my relationships.	A home and community marked by peace, connection, and possibility.	I exist to nurture confidence and belonging in the people I love.

Final Step: Write the One-Line MVP

This is the Athleadership filter.

This is your internal compass.

This is your championship standard.

Template:

My mission is ____

My vision is ____

My purpose is ____

It should fit on the back of an index card.

It should calm you down when the pressure spikes.

It should make hard decisions instantly clearer.

It should feel like the truth—even in its early draft.

Don't chase poetry. Chase the truth. If your voice shakes, good. That means you are hitting something real. Put it where your decisions happen—next to your laptop, on your phone's lock screen, on the cupboard you open at 6:00 a.m.

Then test it—quietly, today. When a shiny request lands, hold it against your line. When you're tempted to overwork to earn your worth, read your line out loud. When you miss or feel small, return to your line and ask, "What's my next step that stays true to this?" That's the practice that turned a torn magazine ad into a global platform and a room full of awake leaders—many of whom began exactly where you're sitting.

You were not born to chase titles until you forget who you are. You were born to condition a way of living and leading that keeps you honest and useful under pressure. That's what a compass does. It doesn't make the storm smaller. It makes *you* steadier. From the copy room to the locker room to boardrooms around the world, this is the throughline: A leader with a clear MVP can walk through grief, change, and growth without losing herself. And when one leader steadies, teams notice. Families notice. Cultures shift. Freedom spreads.

Now it's your turn. Write the line. Put it where you'll see it. And get ready—because somewhere in your week, something will ask, "Are you ready?" You won't feel perfect. You won't feel certain, but you'll have a compass. And that—quietly, consistently—is how movements begin.

Neuroscience Insight: The Power of Purpose on the Brain

Here's what the science tells us: Purpose isn't just good for your soul—it's powerful for your brain. According to a longitudinal study published in *JAMA Network Open*, individuals with a high sense of purpose had a 27 percent lower risk of early death and better cognitive function as they aged.[29] Why?

Because purpose activates the brain's prefrontal cortex, the center for decision-making, focus, and forward planning. In high-pressure environments, the brain defaults to survival mode—*fight*, *flight*, *freeze*, or *fawn*. However, when purpose is activated, it quiets the amygdala and engages the default mode network, allowing for reflection, resilience, and strategic thinking.[30] It creates a neurological filter that helps you make decisions faster, recover stronger, and lead with clarity even under stress. It serves as an anchor to ground you in meaning greater than your current circumstance.

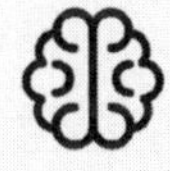

Purpose makes your brain more resilient to pressure. A sense of purpose is linked to lower levels of stress hormone, cortisol, making you less reactive to pressure and giving you greater bounce-back ability in difficult situations.[31] Your MVP isn't just a leadership tool—it's a cognitive advantage.

MVP PULSE CHECK-IN

1. Which part of my MVP feels strongest right now—Mission, Vision, or Purpose?
2. Where am I drifting from what I say matters most?
3. What is one decision I need to realign with my MVP this week?

Keep Going

Revisit your MVP weekly for the next 30 days. Not because your purpose will change, but because you will. The words you originally choose may change . . . many times. This should be expected. Growth clarifies. Awareness sharpens. Honesty refines. It isn't a sentence to admire; it's a compass to *use*. It filters the noise, protects your time, and anchors your choices. It steadies your nervous system when pressure spikes.

When you keep your MVP close—on your desk, your phone, your mirror—it becomes the quiet governor of your life. Not loud, not dramatic, but just steady enough to pull you back into alignment when everything else is screaming with urgency. Urgency will always try to choose your life for you. Your MVP anchors everyday life with intention and focus. And when you inevitably experience a week that tilts sideways—because it will—the question becomes: Does your calendar reflect your compass?

If it's prioritized in your MVP, it must be prioritized in your time. If it's not reflected in your week, something must shift. Delegate, delay, delete, but don't betray your compass to please a moment. This is the shift most leaders never make. They craft a meaningful MVP, then try to live it with an unconditioned mind. That's where overwhelm resurfaces, identity drifts, and pressure wins.

Your MVP is meant to support your decisions, your body, your relationships, your leadership, and your presence. It becomes your compass and your anchor when life gets unsteady. And that requires conditioning in real-time moments that require you to recall your purpose. But your MVP is not the finish line. It is the starting block. It is the essential foundational first step.

Now we begin the real work: building the mental muscle to lead from identity, under pressure, through change, and when it counts.

6

Core 4: Because Conditioning Outperforms Training

"Don't fold under pressure. Great athletes perform better under pressure, so put pressure on yourself."

—Sydney McLaughlin-Levrone, Olympian,
2× World Athlete of the Year

I didn't walk into that first company meeting feeling underqualified, but I felt unprepared. After completing graduate school at Northwestern, I was hired by my next employer under the assumption I would be working in the beauty division because of my prior experience at Victoria's Secret. So, when I landed on the *household cleaning products* division—I quickly realized the language of this world was completely foreign. The meeting began, and suddenly I was underwater. Acronyms flew across the room like code I didn't have the key for. There were category terms, operational jargon, supply-chain shorthand—everyone was speaking a language I didn't know, at a pace I couldn't match. In that moment, I did the only thing I knew how to do: I took notes like my career depended on it.

I scribbled every meeting, every phrase, every acronym into a black faux-leather spiral-bound notebook. Between meetings, I studied my notes. I asked questions. I called colleagues for clarity. I rehearsed my talking points with a coworker, checking my understanding before I ever spoke out loud.

At the next meeting, did I magically get it all? No. But I showed up differently, with one thoughtful question, one strategic observation, or a single step forward.

What I was really building was the mindset and mental stamina to close gaps quickly, stay present under pressure, and perform before I felt ready. My conditioning made me effective long before I felt confident.

Your Brain Is Not Built for Change (But You Can Rewire It)

Before we dive into the Core 4, your conditioning road map, you need to understand the invisible force working against every Athleader under pressure: your biology.[32] Neuroscience confirms that the brain is not wired for change—it is wired for predictability. Any disruption, even a good one, can register as a threat. **Your brain was built to keep you alive, not to help you excel in environments defined by speed, complexity, and constant uncertainty.**

When circumstances shift, when the unexpected hits, when the path ahead blurs, your nervous system reacts long before your strategy can. Your thoughts speed up. Your focus narrows. Your body braces. And your mind defaults to the negative in the absence of information.

When uncertainty increases,

- the amygdala goes into hyper-surveillance;
- cortisol rises;
- the prefrontal cortex—judgment, strategy, emotional regulation—begins to dim;
- creativity collapses;
- reactivity spikes; and
- you cling to familiar habits, even when they no longer serve you.

This is "uncertainty aversion." Your brain would rather grip an old pattern than risk the unknown. But here's what most leaders never learn: Your wiring is not permanent. Your perspective can shift. Your patterns can evolve. Your emotional responses can be reconditioned. Neuroplasticity—the brain's ability to form new pathways—means your relationship to pressure, change, and ambiguity is not fixed.[33]

In fact, the hormesis effect helps the brain accept change by exposing it to new challenges, such as conditioning drills, to learn new skills that build resilience and create new patterns. The conditioning work we will do can help you function better to handle future stress and adapt to new and uncertain situations. This is a form of neuroplasticity. You recondition a brain built for protection. 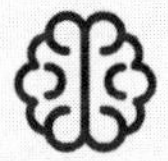

We do it through the same mechanisms elite athletes depend on—awareness that interrupts automatic reactions, reframing that transforms uncertainty into information rather than danger, intentional reps that form new cognitive and emotional habits, novel challenges that stretch capacity, recovery that calms the nervous system, curiosity that dissolves fear, and consistency—the compound interest of high performance. Every time you pause instead of spiraling, you weaken an old loop. Every time you breathe before reacting, you strengthen a new one. Every time you meet uncertainty with inquiry instead of panic, you expand your range.

This is neuroplasticity in motion—activating the brain's seeking system, the network responsible for exploration, learning, and meaning. Curiosity shifts you out of fear and into forward momentum. This is what conditioning is built to do. Because while your brain isn't naturally wired for change, it is wired for growth.

The Core 4 turn growth potential into capability. They are agility, resilience, alignment, and well-being. These are the four mental performance muscles that help you stay grounded, clear, and effective when conditions refuse to cooperate. Your biology explains why you face a challenge, but the Core 4 provide the conditioning to rewire your response.

Agility: Adapt Through Change

Agility is your ability to stay clear, steady, and strategic when the world refuses to cooperate with your plans. It is the mental muscle that allows you to shift from threat-response to thoughtful-response when conditions change without warning. Agility is not speed. It's stability under motion. It's the capacity to regulate your nervous system, update your perspective in real time, and choose your next move with precision rather than panic. In a world where rules change mid-meeting, expectations shift overnight, and uncertainty is the new normal, agility becomes the difference between leaders who react—and Athleaders who respond. Agility helps you move at the speed of change so the pace of the world doesn't drag you through each day.

In neuroscience terms, this helps your prefrontal cortex stay online so you can problem-solve, rather than letting your amygdala take control. Remember that your amygdala directs your fear response, so when that part of your brain directs your behavior, you make reactionary decisions from a place of panic instead of clarity.

Athlete in Action

At the 1996 Atlanta Olympics, Kerri Strug stepped onto the vault with a torn ligament in her ankle and the weight of a nation on her shoulders. After crashing on her first attempt, she had one chance left. She inhaled, recalibrated, and launched—adjusting in midair to protect her injury while still hitting the landing that secured gold for Team USA. What the world remembers is the one-footed landing. What made it possible was her mental agility: the split-second ability to process pain, fear, physics, and pressure—and still choose execution.

Athleader in Action

Sophia, a VP of operations, walked into what she thought was a routine executive meeting, only to learn their largest distribution partner had pulled out of their agreement—effective immediately. She could sense the room tighten as her colleagues braced for impact. Sophia grounded her breath, widened her lens, and reframed the moment: "What options does this create?"

Within minutes, she redirected the agenda, facilitated a rapid strategic huddle, and identified three viable alternate channels. By the end of the day, she had aligned legal, finance, and logistics around a new path forward. Someone on her team later said, "The whole room borrowed her calm." That is an Athleader—someone whose agility becomes a stabilizing force for everyone else.

Your Play: Reflection

Where in your life or leadership are you still reacting to change instead of responding with intention? What would shift if you paused long enough to choose your next move?

Resilience: Champion Under Pressure

Resilience is powered by your recovery capacity—how quickly your nervous system can reset after a stressful event. It is the ability to recalibrate your internal state, and rise with greater clarity after a setback, shock, or emotionally charged moment. It's the mental muscle that determines how quickly you return to presence when pressure tries to pull you into panic, self-doubt, or reactivity. Where agility helps you adapt *in* the moment, resilience helps you rise *after* the moment. It is the discipline of absorbing impact without losing your identity. It allows you to transform adversity into fuel, not fear. Former athletes in executive roles frequently draw on this mental toughness; as noted earlier, they have developed the capacity to recover from setbacks and maintain composure under pressure.[34]

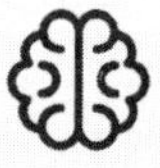
From a neuroscience perspective, resilience depends on *amygdala recovery time*—how quickly your brain's fear center calms after a stress trigger.

Athlete in Action

When Caitlin Clark entered the Women's National Basketball Association (WNBA), she didn't just join a league—she inherited a national spotlight. Before she ever dribbled a professional basketball, she was already carrying expectations no rookie could reasonably shoulder. Every mistake was magnified. Every reaction recorded. Every game, a referendum and a controversy. And yet—she kept showing up. She absorbed criticism, adjusted, learned, and kept performing with precision. She didn't collapse under the weight of her fame and the pressure it brought; she conditioned under it.

What the world witnessed wasn't talent alone. It was resilience in real time, the capacity to stay grounded, recalibrate quickly, and keep moving forward under public pressure.

Athleader in Action

DeShawn, a newly promoted vice president of supply chain, walked into his first major board meeting ready to share the quarter's progress, only to be confronted with an unexpected $18 million revenue loss tied to a supply-chain failure he inherited. Mid-presentation, a board member challenged his readiness for the role.

The room froze. His nervous system surged, but conditioning stepped in. He steadied his breathing, slowed his cadence, and said, "Here's what we've learned, what we've corrected, and what we're doing next." Instead of being defensive, he provided his team with clarity, accountability, and direction. Three months later, the board chair pulled him aside and said, "Your response in that moment earned our trust." That is resilience—not the absence of pressure, but the mastery of recovery.

Your Play: Reflection

Reflect on a rookie season in your life when you faced a new challenge, high expectations, and pressure to perform. When pressure hits, do you bounce back or do you spiral? What would shift if you treated every setback as data used to adjust your next move?

Alignment: Purpose-Driven Performance

Alignment is what happens when your inner purpose and your outer priorities finally agree. It is the mental muscle that brings clarity to chaos, coherence to teams, and direction to ambition. Alignment ensures that your decisions, actions, conversations, and calendar reflect your true mission, vision, and purpose (MVP), not the loudest demand or the nearest fire drill.

Where agility helps you pivot and resilience enables you to recover, alignment helps you *aim*. It is the anchor point that keeps Athleaders from being pulled out of position by pressure, distraction, or urgency. Alignment is not consensus. It is coherence—within yourself and across your team.

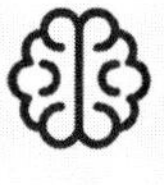 From a neuroscience perspective, these behaviors reduce cognitive load, eliminate decision fatigue, and create shared mental models—the neuroscience of teams that perform with trust and rhythm.

Athlete in Action

If you've ever watched a Division I rowing team glide across the Charles River, you know alignment is not a metaphor but a requirement. There are eight athletes, eight oars, and one rhythm. The difference between surging forward or spinning in circles is alignment, which supports shared timing, shared trust, and shared direction. Alignment is about synchronization. When a crew team rows out of sync, each athlete works harder, but the boat moves more slowly. But when they row as one—clean, unified, intentional—they generate power greater than any individual stroke could deliver. Winning teams aren't always the strongest, but they are the most aligned.

Athleader in Action

Jenna, an HR Athleader, inherited a burned-out team with competing priorities: talent shortages, compliance deadlines, engagement repair, and acquisition of a new business. Everything in her purview was urgent and important, but nothing was coordinated. Everyone was rowing as fast as they could, but no one was rowing together.

Instead of adding another initiative, she called for a department reset. She guided the team through mapping their personal MVPs, clarifying the department's mission, eliminating work that didn't serve it, and building a shared 12-month vision with clear priorities and boundaries, identifying what each team member would be accountable for and how the team would collaborate to deliver against the top priorities.

Within 30 days,

- Meetings shortened.
- Redundancies disappeared.
- Conflicts eased.
- Collaboration accelerated.

One analyst said, "It finally feels like we're moving in the same direction." That is alignment—clarity that becomes momentum.

Your Play: Reflection

Where in your leadership are you moving fast but not in the direction that reflects purposeful impact? What one shift would bring you back into alignment for yourself and/or those around you (team, family, etc.)?

Well-Being: Sustainable Energy Performance

Well-being is not relaxation, self-care, or reward. It is an energy strategy that supports the disciplined, intentional management of your physical, mental, spiritual, and emotional capacity so you can perform at a high level *reliably*, not occasionally. Chronic stress keeps cortisol high, impairing memory, decision-making, and emotional regulation. Athleaders understand that pressure isn't the enemy; depletion is. Well-being is the mental muscle that protects your clarity, amplifies your creativity, and safeguards the resilience and agility you've worked so hard to build. It is what allows you to show up strong not once, but again and again, in the moments that count. Sustainable performance requires a sustainable you, and well-being is the system that makes that possible.

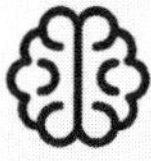 From a neuroscience lens, well-being optimizes prefrontal cortex functioning, lowers cortisol, improves memory consolidation, and strengthens emotional regulation. These are all essential for leading under prolonged pressure.

Athlete in Action

At the height of his career, I worked with one of the NBA's most dominant forwards, a ten-time All-Star athlete. The kind of competitor you'd expect to be grinding nonstop.

One afternoon, mid-season, I called to check in. His assistant answered: "He's taking a nap."

What I didn't understand then—but know now—is that world-class athletes are disciplined about recovery. Sleep, nutrition, stretching, treatments, rest cycles, strategic downtime—all of it is performance preparation. Peak performance oscillates. Even champions conserve and restore energy. Elite athletes don't wait to crash before they recover. They recover to avoid the crash.

Athleader in Action

Marcus, a top-performing engineer Athleader, was the kind of leader companies highlight at awards dinners. He was the first in the office and the last one out. He was always available, always *on*, until his body quit. He had heart palpitations, short-term memory lapses, and bone-deep exhaustion. He was emotionally volatile.

A performance coach told him what no one else had the courage to say: "You're not burned out because you're weak. You're burned out because you've been performing without recovery."

Marcus began practicing 90-second box breathing (deep inhale for four seconds and deep exhale for four seconds) before major calls, instituted two nonnegotiable recovery blocks per week, and enforced "no meeting Fridays" for his team to focus on deep work. Within a quarter, his productivity increased significantly. His team became sharper, calmer, more consistent. Well-being didn't make him softer. It made him more strategic.

That is the power of well-being—an energy system that fuels longevity, quality, and clarity.

Your Play: Reflection

If your energy is the engine of your leadership, what habit, boundary, or recovery practice must you put in place now to protect the performance you're expecting from yourself?

The Integrated Athleader

The Core 4 gives you something most leaders never have: visibility into what's happening inside you while you're moving through change. Instead of reacting blindly to pressure, you begin to recognize the shifts—your thoughts, your energy, your focus—and you learn how to work with them, not against them. It's the inner mechanics of leading well. Athleaders place a premium value on the process, not just the prize of achievement. When agility, resilience, alignment, and well-being start working together, you begin to see your own patterns more clearly. You get better at catching yourself, correcting course, and staying grounded, even when things around you are moving. You can lead yourself and your team through change with more honesty, strength, and intention, and build the kind of character you can sustain.

Conditioning in Action Live on CNN

The lights hit me first, hot and unforgiving. They made the situation feel more like an interrogation than an illumination. Every bead of sweat felt like it was on broadcast delay, magnified for the world to see. I was invited to be a guest on CNN to give my expert take on the NFL player for the Baltimore Ravens, Ray Rice's domestic violence incident. In times of crisis, I would often be asked to join live to share my take on the hot topic in the news regarding brands, leadership, and sports. The cameras locked on me, and the red ON AIR sign glowed and a CNN producer's voice crackled through my earpiece. *"We're live in three . . . two . . ."*

This wasn't my first time in the arena. I'd been invited to CNN and other news outlets as an expert to analyze cultural and business crises live in studio for moments such as when Penn State fired its coaching staff citing sexual assault charges, Tiger Woods's affair scandal, the

NBA's social media comments about China, and more. In this instance, it was the NFL and the Ray Rice domestic violence crisis—a cultural flashpoint with careers, reputations, fans, and millions in sponsorships at stake. My talking points were razor-sharp. Years of working with athletes and executives in high-stakes moments had prepared me for this. This was supposed to be a one-on-one, so I expected it to feel controlled and measured.

I was mid-thought, laser-focused on the anchor, when I heard the words: "Let's bring in legal expert, Mel Robbins." Mel Robbins—as in *the* Mel Robbins. At the time, Mel wasn't the household name she is today for *Let Them* and *The 5-Second Rule*, but she was a respected CNN legal commentator with a commanding presence, sharp insights, and the kind of debate skills that can flip a segment in an instant. Suddenly, this was no longer a controlled interview. It was a live point-counterpoint with a seasoned legal mind whose cadence alone could disarm an unready guest, and I had just ten seconds to get ready.

My brain flickered through options like rapid-fire frames: *Do I adjust my tone? Stay on message? Engage? Defend?* My heart rate spiked. My breath tightened. In my head, I heard my own voice: *You've got this.* The segment began and we were live. Mel spoke—clear, commanding, sharp. I listened, not just to her words, but to the tempo, the pauses, the openings. This wasn't about competing; it was about contributing—and doing it in a way that honored my perspective while respecting hers.

In those minutes, everything slowed. I could feel myself shifting gears. Time seemed to slow as my focus narrowed. I prepared to let my conditioning do the work.

- **Agility:** Shifting instantly from solo delivery to a dynamic exchange
- **Resilience:** Staying anchored in my expertise, even when the narrative tilted

- **Alignment:** Speaking from the center of my core truth, not from ego
- **Well-being:** Keeping my breath steady, my voice calm, my energy sustainable under the weight of the lights

This was about composure under unexpected pressure. I had to adapt without losing the core of my message. I had to regulate my own nervous system in real time to keep my prefrontal cortex online while the pressure tried to hijack it. I had to keep my answers grounded in the mission for which I was there. I had to manage my energy to sustain clarity throughout the entire segment. Every word was intentional. Every pause had to project confidence, not hesitation. When the red ON AIR light finally blinked off, I exhaled. I didn't know how it would play in the headlines, but I knew this: I had stayed in the game.

That day taught me a truth I didn't have language for yet: Moments like these aren't decided by talent alone—or even preparation in the traditional sense. They're decided by *conditioning*.

Because you can't predict every curveball. But you can condition yourself to meet it without losing your center. And that's exactly what the Core 4 is built to do.

Training Versus Conditioning: Why Readiness Decides Who Performs When It Counts

In sports, training sharpens skills. You run drills, refine your technique, and memorize plays. Skills are essential. Without them, you cannot even get on the field. But skills alone do not determine who wins when the clock is winding down, the crowd is roaring, and the stakes could not be higher. Conditioning is different. It is what shows up when you are at bat in the final game of the World Series. It is the invisible work that prepares you to perform when skill is no longer enough, when fatigue sets in, when the plan breaks down, and when the unexpected blindsides you.

Professional athletes are paid a premium not simply for their talent, but for their ability to perform under pressure when the moment is unforgiving and the outcome matters. The same principle applies to leadership. Many capable people can deliver when conditions are favorable, but those who can think clearly, stay composed, and execute when stakes are high become the leaders others rely on. That reliability creates opportunity, influence, and career momentum. Over time, your ability to perform under pressure becomes part of your professional reputation. It signals that you can be trusted with bigger decisions, greater responsibility, and more visible roles. This is where potential turns into value. When you condition yourself to perform when it counts, you are not just growing as a leader. You are increasing your worth in any environment that depends on sound judgment and steady execution.

As former NFL Dallas Cowboys player Roger Staubach put it: **"All of us get knocked down, but it's resiliency that really matters. All of us do well when things are going well, but the thing that distinguishes athletes is the ability to do well in times of great stress, urgency, and pressure."**

TRAINING	CONDITIONING
Learns the play	Becomes the instinct
Cognitive	Neurobiological
Skill acquisition	Response shaping
Conscious effort	Automatic execution
Prefrontal cortex–driven	Nervous system integrated
Practiced in stability	Revealed under pressure
Knowledge-based	Identity-level

Training prepares you for the plan. Conditioning prepares you for the moment.

The Process of Becoming: How Conditioning Rewires Through Change

The breaking, the shifting, and the shaping all come by process. If you look back, you are stronger because of the challenges you have faced. Now you understand the Core 4, the four mental performance muscles every Athleader must condition. But muscles don't grow because you admire them. They grow because you condition them through the pain, discomfort, and challenges you have had to overcome.

The Conditioning System— The Becoming Process

Conditioning is the bridge between who you are today and the Athleader you're becoming.

It is the process that makes the Core 4 live in your everyday life—in your inbox, at your kitchen counter, on the 7:00 a.m. call that goes sideways, during the 11:47 p.m. email that spikes your adrenaline, and in the quiet moments when life demands a deeper strength from you.

Conditioning has four elements that work together to rewire your brain: drills, reps, rhythm, and recovery.

Drills: How You Practice Under Pressure

The purpose of drills is to practice the Core 4 so you can build your skills. Drills are short, simple, repeatable tools that strengthen a specific Core 4 muscle, the Athleader equivalent of practicing free throws, footwork, or starts out of the blocks.

Drills train your brain for the moment pressure hits by converting insight into instinct, awareness into action, and theory into muscle memory.

Reps: What You Repeat

Reps are the micro-behaviors you practice consistently until they become automatic. A rep can be

- Pausing 60 seconds before responding
- Taking one deep breath before speaking
- Asking "What's the next best step?" instead of spiraling
- Ending your day by naming one win and one thing you learned

These small actions interrupt the stress response, activate the prefrontal cortex, and slowly build new neural pathways. Reps wire the mindset and build your leadership reflex, like an athlete practicing their free-throw technique.

Rhythm: When and How Often You Repeat It

Rhythm is your cadence. Champions don't train randomly; they train rhythmically. For Athleaders, rhythm looks like

- A morning reset to get your head in alignment
- A weekly MVP check-in
- Friday reflections on drift and direction
- Monthly energy resets
- Seasonal recalibration during life's tides

Rhythm creates predictability for the brain and stabilizes your internal world during external change.

Recovery: How You Restore Energy

Recovery isn't an indulgence; it is performance infrastructure. Your brain cannot stay in decision-making mode without rest. Recovery practices—micro and macro—lower cortisol, restore cognitive capacity, and bring your nervous system back to center.

Recovery looks like

- A five-minute walk before a difficult call
- 90-second breathing between meetings
- Shutting down screens before bed
- One boundary you protect no matter what

Recovery makes performance repeatable.

As leaders practiced the Core 4 over a 90-day cycle, the most meaningful shifts did not appear as dramatic breakthroughs. They appeared as quieter, more durable changes in how leaders operated under pressure. Across cohorts, leaders reported faster recovery after setbacks, greater clarity in decision-making, and a reduced tendency to default to urgency as a leadership style. These shifts were not tied to learning more content. They were tied to conditioning how leaders responded in moments that mattered. The data reinforced a critical distinction: Training improved awareness; conditioning changed behavior. When leaders strengthened agility, resilience, alignment, and well-being together, performance stabilized—not because demands lessened but because capacity increased.

My goal is for you to learn the mental conditioning model that makes you a modern leader who performs under pressure, leads through change, and stays grounded no matter what the moment demands.

In the next chapters, we begin the real work of conditioning with small, science-backed practices that engage the mind, starting with the first of the Core 4.

7

Agility: What to Do When the Ground Beneath You Shifts

On Wednesday, March 11, 2020, the World Health Organization declared COVID-19 a global pandemic. Two days later, my company, Velvet Suite, was supposed to host the biggest live She-Suite Summit we had ever produced at the Ritz-Carlton in Tyson's Corner, Virginia. It had taken months of preparation. We had sponsors committed and a ballroom shimmering with expectation. My team and I were at the hotel for final setup when the world seemed to exhale and stop.

I remember standing in the conference room with the hotel executives who met my passionate optimism with the stark reality: This Summit was shut down. The air was thick with anticipation and dread, and I was feeling the ground of my certainty shift beneath my feet. It was as if time paused long enough for me to feel the full weight of what was unfolding. Every instinct in me wanted clarity, control, a plan to cling to—but none of those existed anymore.

I stepped out of the room and found the quietest corner I could—a service hallway near the hotel kitchens—and I prayed. Not for things to go back to the way they were, but for discernment. For wisdom. For the courage to release the plan I'd built so carefully, and trust that something else—something unplanned and unexpected—might still be possible. To let go of the fear of failure, disappointment, and everyone's expectations of me.

When I opened my eyes, nothing in the world had changed, but something inside me had. My fear didn't disappear, but it loosened its grip. My job wasn't to control the storm; it was to anchor myself inside it. I realized that my team would follow my energy and my lead. I settled this decision in my heart. We will go forward. I walked back into that ballroom and told my team the truth: "We're not canceling. We're pivoting. The vision continues. Are you in?"

Without a road map, a playbook, or comfort, our talented team was all in. They brought their purpose and conviction. We were resolved to be a source of strength in a moment when the world stood still. We leaned into our vision and supported each other through the unknown.

We locked ourselves in that hotel and rebuilt a nine-hour live summit into a fully virtual experience in less than 38 hours. I'm convinced we were among the very first to pioneer virtual events during the global pandemic. We storyboarded, rewired logistics, coached speakers, reimagined engagement, and stitched together an event that should have taken months—overnight. Was it polished? No. Was it perfect? Not even close. Was it possible? Absolutely.

And what happened next still astonishes me. What began as a national gathering became a global movement. Over the next five years of the She-Suite Summit virtual experience, Velvet Suite would host thousands of leaders across more than 40 countries, expanding our vision far beyond anything I could have planned. The pivot born in panic became the breakthrough that would reshape our entire platform.

People ask me what that moment taught me about leadership. It taught me this: Agility isn't speed, but surrender. It's the sacred pause where you stop clinging to what was and make space for what could be.

At that moment, agility wasn't a strategy. It was obedience. It was trust. It was the willingness to release my grip long enough for God to redirect my steps, a sacred vow I made within my own mission statement. That pivot became one of the clearest mirrors of my own wiring—and one of the greatest rewiring moments of my life. It taught me that the future doesn't always arrive the way you planned, but it will always meet you where you're willing to pivot.

The leaders who rise aren't the ones who hold on the tightest, but are the ones who release quickly, listen deeply, and move wisely. They become the leader the moment demands.

The Premise

Most people treat change like an interruption. But for an Athleader, change is initiation. It's the invitation to practice a deeper presence, to access a wiser part of yourself, to quiet the noise long enough to hear what the moment is asking of you. It's a moment to elevate your value and impact. That night before the Summit went virtual, I wasn't performing agility—I was remembering it. Returning to it. Regrounding myself inside the identity I had spent years building. Agility is not a strategy; it is a state of being. It is the first mental muscle of Athleadership because everything else flows from it.

The Muscle: Agility

Agility is the discipline of adapting under pressure by staying mentally flexible, emotionally steady, and open to possibility. It is the mental muscle that allows you to regulate your nervous system under pressure, keep your prefrontal cortex online, and adapt through change without abandoning your purpose. Agility is not speed; it is stability in motion, the discipline of shifting wisely, pivoting intentionally, and choosing your next move with clarity rather than panic. It is how leaders remain themselves in the very moments that demand the most of them.

Most people think agility is a personality trait, something you either have or you don't. But agility is a conditioned capability. It's the inner stability that allows you to update your perspective in real time, regulate your nervous system under pressure, and choose your next move with clarity instead of fear.

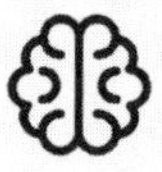 In neuroscience terms, agility is what happens when you're able to keep your prefrontal cortex online—the part of your brain responsible for problem-solving, emotional regulation, and strategic thinking—rather than being overtaken by the amygdala, which screams *danger* even when the danger is only uncertainty.[35]

When you can interrupt that hijacking, even briefly, you unlock your ability to think, see, choose, and lead.

Agility lives through **three performance capacities** that together create your internal agility architecture. The first is cognitive flexibility, the ability to reroute, reinterpret, and reframe when reality shifts. It's what allows you to pivot without losing purpose, to see possibilities where others only see disruption, and to adapt without abandoning what matters. The second is emotional agility under stress, the ability to regulate your internal world before your internal world derails your external leadership. This is the skill that keeps your breath steady when the stakes rise, tempers your tone when emotions flare, and brings you back to presence so you can lead from discernment rather than fear. The third is decision-making in ambiguity, the ability to choose direction when the data is incomplete, the path is unclear, and certainty is nowhere in sight. This is the heart of modern leadership: the willingness to move forward when you can't guarantee the outcome.

When these three capacities work together, something powerful happens. You become calm in the chaos. The anchor in motion. The person people look to when everything feels unstable—not because you have all the answers, but because you aren't undone by the unknown.

Agility doesn't eliminate uncertainty; it transforms your relationship to it. Instead of resisting change, you learn to work with it. Instead of bracing for impact, you learn to bend with intention. Instead of freezing, you find the next intelligent move. This is the muscle every modern leader must build—not to outrun change but to meet it with clarity, courage, and composure.

The Gap: Where Agility Breaks Down When Pressure Shows Up

Imagine a morning when you open your laptop and the first email hits you sideways, knocks the wind out of you before you've even had a chance to settle into your day. You weren't trying to panic. You weren't trying to freeze. But something in you tightened. Your breath shortened. Your mind tried to make sense of the shift, and before you could catch yourself, you were already reacting from the place you swore you'd evolved beyond. Or maybe it showed up in a meeting where a conversation veered off-course, where someone said something that caught you unprepared. And you felt your entire system do what human systems do—default to defensiveness, shutting down, racing forward, and filling the silence with more words than clarity.

Suddenly, the version of you that feels strong and capable in one area of life disappears in another. Not because you're weak, but because your nervous system doesn't care if the disruption is professional or personal. It reacts to threat, not context.

If any of this feels familiar, you are not alone. You're human. And humans struggle with agility not because we lack discipline—but because pressure rearranges our internal world before we realize it's happening. Every one of us knows what it feels like to want to respond with clarity—and instead feel our mind clutter itself with what-ifs, worst-case scenarios, or that familiar inner critic who always seems to raise her voice at the exact wrong time. These are all signals that the muscle of agility is calling you to strengthen it, not to judge yourself for the moments you weren't able to. You don't rise to the best version of yourself when uncertainty hits—you rise to the level of the agility you've conditioned.

The Science: What Your Brain Is Doing in the Moment Your Agility Is Tested

If you've ever wondered why a simple change—a shift in tone from your boss, a sudden update to a project, a meeting that takes an unexpected turn—can rattle you more than you'd like to admit, the reason isn't personal weakness. It's biology. Long before you open your mouth or decide what to do next, your brain has already made a calculation about what's happening. And it doesn't ask your permission.

Your brain is designed to keep you safe, not to keep you agile. For all the sophistication of your degrees, your experience, your title, your intuition—there is a part of you still wired like your ancestors were. They walked through life scanning for danger. And though your "danger" looks different now, your brain has not evolved nearly as fast as your environment has. Your amygdala—the brain's threat detection center—doesn't differentiate between a predator in the bushes and a PowerPoint slide that contradicts your data.[36] It reacts the same way: fast, protective, absolute.

Your body responds before you do—your breath grows shallow, your muscles brace, your hearing sharpens, your thinking narrows. You might feel a ping of defensiveness or a rush of urgency. You may even feel yourself disconnect from your calm, grounded center. And then you wonder, *Why did I react that way? I know better.* Here's the answer: You reacted because your nervous system responded to a version of danger you didn't consciously choose. But you can condition that system to respond differently.

While the amygdala fires first, it doesn't have to fire last. There is another part of your brain—the prefrontal cortex—that steps into the moment like a wise counselor. It slows things down. It sorts through options. It helps you weigh consequences. It manages your tone, your clarity, your decisions, and your emotional steadiness. Think about the moments when you have been at your best—present, grounded, able to pivot without losing your center. In those moments, your brain wasn't calm because circumstances were calm.

This is why leaders who seem "naturally calm under pressure" aren't actually natural. They are conditioned to buy time in that gap. You've done this too—even if you didn't know it at the time. Perhaps you've forced yourself to breathe before responding or chosen to ask one clarifying question instead of reacting. In those moments, you catch yourself and pull back your focus instead of spiraling. Every one of those moments made the prefrontal cortex a little stronger, gave the amygdala a little less control, and showed your nervous system that you can bend without breaking, pivot without panicking, adjust without abandoning yourself.

This is the science of agility: You are training your brain to stay present long enough to access the grounded, wise, steady version of you—the one who doesn't disappear when the moment shifts. When you understand this, something inside you softens, and you stop judging yourself for your reactions or expecting perfection. Instead, you begin to see agility for what it is: a trainable capacity and a renewable mental muscle you can condition.

Once you understand what your brain is doing—and how to work with it rather than against it—you gain access to a level of leadership grounded not in habit but in choice.

Athlete in Action:
Olympic Champion Simone Biles and the Split-Second Pivot

There is a moment burned into the memory of anyone who watched the Tokyo Olympics unfold in real time—one of those moments when the entire world seemed to inhale at once, suspended between disbelief and recognition. Simone Biles sprinted down the runway for what should have been a vault she had completed thousands of times in practice, a movement so deeply encoded into muscle memory it lived somewhere below conscious thought. And yet, in mid-air, something ruptured—an internal disorientation gymnasts call *the twisties*, a sudden neurological break between intention and execution where the brain quite literally loses track of the body in space.

In that fraction of a second, Simone found herself suspended between danger and possibility, between what was expected of her and what her own nervous system was capable of giving. She landed—somehow—on her feet, her body absorbing a shock that could have ended her career in an instant. But it was what happened *after* the landing that revealed the deeper truth.

Biles walked off the mat not as a superstar fighting to preserve a medal, but as a human being whose brain had hit its threshold for pressure. She felt the world watching—coaches, teammates, commentators, millions of fans—and still made the decision that would redefine courage on the global stage. She withdrew. Not out of fear, but out of profound clarity. She understood that one more vault attempted in that neurological state could cost her everything.

That decision, that quiet pivot away from expectation and toward truth, was agility in its highest form. Because agility is not the thrill of the perfect landing—it is the discernment to recognize when continuing the same path will cause harm. It is the ability to feel the body's alarm bells, listen to what the nervous system is saying, and reorient— even when everything around you is demanding performance.

What was happening with Biles was one of the most extraordinary displays of cognitive flexibility under pressure we have ever witnessed: a young woman overriding the cultural script to push through, interrupting her own threat-response, and choosing a different move in real time. Neuroscience tells us that when the amygdala fires intensely enough, it disrupts proprioception, perception, and sequencing—exactly what "the twisties" are. At that moment, Biles's brain was trying to protect her, not sabotage her. Her choice to step back was not a collapse—it was a recalibration, a refusal to let pressure override presence.

Later, when she returned to competition, she didn't return to prove anything to anyone. She returned because she had regained the internal alignment required to perform safely, grounded, and with integrity. And when she took that bronze medal on balance beam—an event she reentered on her own terms—it wasn't a consolation prize. It was the embodied reminder that sometimes agility is not performing through the storm, but knowing when to pause long enough to let the storm inside you settle.

Simone Biles showed the world that agility isn't simply reacting quickly—it's responding wisely. It's the courage to pivot before the fall, the clarity to honor your limits, and the strength to rewrite the narrative mid-flight. For leaders, for anyone navigating change, this is the model: agility as a lived, internal discipline—one that protects your future, honors your humanity, and ultimately allows you to rise again with intention rather than compulsion.

Athleader in Action:
What Bracken Darrell, CEO, VF Corporation Taught Me About Agility

When I had Bracken Darrell on my podcast, I expected brilliance. What I didn't expect was to walk away feeling like I had just been coached—personally—on what true agility looks like in a leader who refuses to be defined by yesterday.

Sitting with Bracken, I realized I wasn't interviewing a typical CEO; I was sitting with someone who treats reinvention as a daily discipline. He told me that leaders must "get back to zero," his way of describing the courage to strip away everything you think you know so you can see the world—and yourself—with beginner's eyes again. It wasn't theory. It was the foundation of how he leads. And when you look at his track record, the proof is undeniable. At the time as CEO of Logitech, he didn't just optimize an existing business model—he *reimagined* it. He turned a traditional tech peripherals company into a powerhouse design brand, quadrupling profits and reshaping its identity with a level of creativity most leaders never attempt. That is agility—not the ability to turn fast, but the ability to turn true.

Today, as CEO of VF Corporation, Bracken continues that same pattern of thoughtful, relentless transformation. He is steering some of the world's most iconic lifestyle brands through the turbulence of a shifting consumer culture—using the same mindset he taught me on the podcast: stay humble, stay curious, stay willing to disrupt your own thinking before the world does it for you.

What struck me most wasn't the scale of his results. It was the character underneath them. He reads deeply. He likes to play basketball several times a week. He is a lifelong learner who refuses to let his expertise fossilize into ego. He once "fired himself" from his own mental model of leadership after reading *Thinking, Fast and Slow*—because he realized reinvention isn't an event; it's a rhythm.

In a world where change has become the constant and certainty the exception, Bracken models the posture of an Athleader—someone whose clarity emerges not from knowing everything, but from staying open enough to see what others miss.

The Reflection

Agility becomes real the moment life stops cooperating with your script. And if you're honest, you've had more of those moments than you've admitted out loud. The detour you didn't plan. The silence you didn't expect. The curveball that arrived on a Sunday afternoon and knocked the confidence right out of your chest. You know what it feels like when your breath shortens, your mind tightens, and suddenly the thing you thought you had control over slips.

I want you to pause here—not to judge yourself, but to observe yourself. Think back to a recent moment when change surprised you, challenged you, or confronted you. Maybe it was the meeting that turned sideways without warning. Maybe it was the conversation you replayed a hundred times on the drive home. Maybe it was the email that shifted your plans in an instant.

When the moment changed, did you? Or did you freeze inside the version of you that felt safest?

That's the question agility forces you to face. Not whether you knew what to do. Not whether you had enough information. But whether you gave yourself permission to adapt—quickly, quietly, courageously—even when your certainty collapsed.

Here's the truth most leaders never whisper: You don't lose your edge because of change. You lose it because you try to lead with yesterday's reflexes.

Where in your life are you still reacting to change instead of responding to it—and what would shift if you gave yourself ten extra seconds of breath, clarity, and choice before moving?

↺ AGILITY PULSE CHECK-IN

1. Where am I resisting a change I already know is happening?
2. What story am I telling myself that is keeping me stuck?
3. What is one small move I can make today to respond instead of react?

The Drill: Reset
(5 Words → 2 Options → 1 Default)

I want to return to the hallway of that hotel where the world shifted beneath my feet. I didn't know it then, but everything I teach in this book—the Core 4, the conditioning model, the becoming process—was already alive inside me. I was not just making a decision. I was running a drill I had unknowingly rehearsed for years.

What a Drill Is (and Why It Matters)

A drill is not a concept. It's not a mindset. It's not a motivational line to pin on your wall. A drill is a *micro-tool*—a short, repeatable action that interrupts your stress response and reengages your ability to think clearly under pressure. It is the mental equivalent of an athlete practicing footwork, free throws, or starts out of the blocks.

It's the smallest, most essential form of conditioning.

HOW TO CHOOSE YOUR FIVE WORDS

Your five words are not positive thinking. They are not meant to inspire you. They are meant to regulate you. To create your five words, ask two questions, which is our foundational Reset Drill:

1. **What does my mind need to hear to stop spiraling?**
   - Agility: "I'm not in danger—deciding."
     (5 words, 2 options, 1 default)
   - Resilience: "I bend; I don't break."
     (5 words, 2 truths, 1 choice)
   - Alignment: "Return to what matters now."
     (5 words, 2 truths, 1 promise)
   - Well-being: "Slow down; come back home."
     (5 words, 2 boundaries, 1 reset)

2. **What do I need to remember to reengage in this high-stakes moment?**

The Foundation Reset Drill

A signature, system-wide drill for Athleadership. It helps restore executive function under pressure. It's designed to interrupt the hijacking of your mind when choosing the next step.

5 Words → 2 Options → 1 Default

Here's how it works:

STEP ❶: **5 Words**	Say (out loud or silently): **"I'm not in danger—deciding."** These five words send a signal to your amygdala: *Stand down.* And a signal to your prefrontal cortex: *Come back online.*
STEP ❷: **2 Options**	Ask: **"What are two next-best steps?"** Not ten options. Not the perfect option. Just two. Just two. Two opens choice without overwhelming the brain. This gives you agency.
STEP ❸: **1 Default**	Pick **one action** you will take in the next ten minutes. This snaps your brain out of paralysis and into motion.

How It Lived Inside My 38-Hour Pivot

When the world shut down, and our largest summit was two days away, I stepped into that hallway with a thousand questions and one truth: I had to choose who I was going to be in that moment. I didn't have time to panic or spiral. I had prepared for a room full of leaders whose lives were about to be changed—and a global shutdown that threatened to silence everything we had built.

So I used the Reset without knowing its name.

The 5 Words hit first.

A grounding whisper: "I'm not in danger—deciding."

The fear quieted just enough for clarity to surface.

Then the 2 Options:

"Cancel or pivot?"

Both were possible. Only one aligned with purpose.

And then the 1 Default:

"We pivot. Now."

That decision—one default move—carried us into a 38-hour sprint that birthed one of the first global virtual leadership events of the pandemic, ultimately reaching thousands of leaders across more than 40 countries.

That day, agility wasn't speed, but surrender, clarity, obedience to purpose, and the courage to choose forward motion even when the world froze.

The Practice: Your Agility Drill in Action

It's time for practice. Think about a moment that tested your agility in the recent past, one that is happening as we speak. I want to invite you to use the conditioning framework below to go through this exercise:

Pause + Reset (*Drill*)

Say the five words. Feel your breath return. This is your safety signal.

Identify Two Options (*Rep*)

"What two next-best steps could I take?"

Choose One (*Rhythm*)

Pick one move in the next ten minutes.

Anchor Before Action (*Recovery*)

Take one deep, slow inhale. Step forward.

This is not a checklist; it is a way of being. And it is how you start becoming the kind of leader who adapts, steadies, pivots, and chooses presence over panic.

The Integration

Agility is the first step toward living your mission, vision, and purpose (MVP). It is the one mental muscle that meets you at the doorway of every unexpected moment, every disrupted plan, and every turning point that asks more of you than you were prepared to give. It's the muscle that kept me anchored in that hotel ballroom in March 2020, when the world fractured in real time and I had to choose—panic or pivot, clench or create, freeze or follow faith. And just like that moment invited me into a deeper becoming, every moment of change in your life is asking you to do the same. When your agility strengthens, resilience helps you recover, alignment sharpens your focus, and well-being becomes something more than maintenance—it becomes your quiet power source. Agility is not about becoming faster; it's about becoming clearer. It's the muscle that teaches you to breathe during the storm instead of waiting for the sky to calm. And as you've seen in the stories throughout this chapter, agility is built, conditioned, and practiced in real time. It emerges in times of real fear, when there are cracks between what you expected and what you are facing. This is the muscle that begins to remake you from the inside out, the one that teaches you how to lead when certainty disappears and the familiar no longer fits. And now that you have felt it—now that you've learned its rhythm and recognized its invitation—you are ready for the next step in this becoming. Turn the page. Let's build resilience.

8

Resilience: Lose No Lessons

"I've missed more than 9,000 shots in my career. I've lost almost 300 games. 26 times, I've been trusted to take the game-winning shot and missed. I've failed over and over and over again in my life. And that is why I succeed."

—Michael Jordan, 6x NBA Champion and NBA Hall of Famer

There are moments in life when the plans you've held close—plans you thought were aligned, ordained, and unfolding on schedule—shatter without warning. I was in my early twenties when my boyfriend, Jason, died suddenly. A game of pick-up basketball at a local gym in Chicago led to cardiac arrhythmia, which ended his life at age 27. One phone call split my world in two, dividing my life into *before* and *after*. Grief wasn't an emotion—it was an atmosphere. It rearranged my soul and left me with pieces I no longer recognized.

People tried to encourage me with words like *strength* and *resilience*, but I didn't feel strong. What I felt was broken open. And yet, in the rawness of that season, something quietly faithful began to take shape. The pain didn't disappear, but it began to pay me—slowly, strangely, redemptively. Velvet Suite was born in that space between mess and meaning. I didn't start a company; I started searching for my why. I wanted to rebuild a life that felt aligned, purposeful, and whole.

But grief isn't the only place resilience is required. Healing takes time, intention, and courage. My journey stretched out for 11 years—years of pouring into my business, growing, leading, traveling, laughing, praying, and trying to date with a heart still learning how to trust again. There was a pillow on my bed that said, *How many frogs do I have to kiss?* I still believe it was prophetic, and possibly a threat.

People asked me constantly, "How are you still single?" They meant it kindly, but it landed like a stone. After a while, even I wondered: *Is love still for me? Has too much time passed? Am I the common denominator?* I realized I had made space for everything—my purpose, my team, my calling—but not for love. I had been waiting for it to arrive, with no-where to land.

I resolved to become intentional about allowing love into my life. I wasn't desperate or hurried, but determined to make an effort and a difference. I wrote myself a 90-day plan of action to make my per-sonal life a priority—not to find love, but to become spacious enough to receive it. I practiced going to dinner solo to rediscover who I was. I cooked meals for one with ceremony and joy. I read books like *Get-ting to "I Do"* by Dr. Patricia Allen. I made a list of over 75 attributes that I believed my future husband would have, not as a checklist, but as a thoughtful representation of the kind of alignment that mattered to me. I conditioned myself to soften, to open, to hope again. I got feedback that I needed to appear more approachable. So, shopping one day, I came across this simple black t-shirt that said, "Never Stop Smil-ing Because Someone Will Always Fall in Love with Your Smile." Ten bucks later, the shirt was mine. I was practicing being open. And when I finally told my friends, with absolute conviction, "This is my last single summer," they laughed. I laughed too. But something in me had shifted from longing to readiness.

On a Friday in October, I was out at a party with some girlfriends. On my way to the bathroom, a guy stopped me to offer his opinion, announcing, "Hey, how are you? You should smile." It was a corny pickup line, but he wasn't the first person to give me that feedback (hence the shirt). His words triggered a gentle reminder, and I *smiled*. While he was trying to flirt, another man walked behind him and caught a glimpse of my smile. The second man, who was strikingly tall, caught my eye—as if we were old friends—and made the gesture of dragging his finger across his throat. Shaking his head from side to side, he was signaling, "Not this guy. Come talk to me."

That conversation led to talking until 6:00 a.m. and having breakfast at IHOP. Struck by the coincidence of it all, I asked him what made him approach me. "I saw you smile," he said. Six weeks later, I was engaged to the fine six-foot-seven giant, and we were married nine months after that. Today, Will Simkins is my husband and my purpose partner.

Resilience didn't bring me Will, but it made me ready for him. It restored my capacity to believe in a life I could not yet see. It taught me that loss can break your heart, but it does not get to break your becoming. It revealed that the timeline you want isn't always the timeline you need. I begin this chapter not with theory, but with truth lived in the tender spaces. Because resilience isn't the polished, curated narrative people admire from afar. It's the gritty, honest work of rebuilding yourself in the quiet hours when no one is watching. Resilience is the sacred strength that allows you to rise—not because the pain vanished, but because purpose kept calling. It is the spiritual elasticity that lets you stay soft without falling apart, the inner anchor that whispers, *This is not how your story ends.*

Resilience awakened a muscle in me, and it will do the same for you, helping you strengthen the parts where your own life has stretched you thin.

The Premise

Before we break open the mechanics of resilience, I want to honor the truth that sits quietly beneath every comeback you have ever had to make: Resilience is not the strength to push through; it is the grace to rise through. It's the slow, persistent work of rebuilding a self after life has broken your heart, rearranged your plans, or rewritten the future you thought you were walking toward.

Most people misunderstand resilience. They think it's grit or toughness or the ability to "keep going." But resilience has far more depth—and far more softness—than that. **Resilience is the willingness to keep becoming when life has taken something from you.** It's the courage to confront the emptiness, to tell the truth about the ache, to choose hope when hopelessness feels easier, and to open your heart again even though the last time cost you dearly.

When I look back at those 11 years—the loss, the loneliness, the questions, the prayers, the summer I finally declared I was making room for love—I understand now that resilience wasn't something I mastered. It was something being formed within me, shaping me slowly and deeply, preparing me not just to receive love but to hold it, honor it, and rise to it.

Resilience is the muscle that rebuilds your internal world after life rearranges your external one. It is the quiet architect of strength, the keeper of hope, the restorer of identity. And just like agility, resilience is conditioned and practiced. It's something you build, not some theory you learn about. You are not here to study resilience. You are here to reclaim the parts of you that hardship tried to take.

The Muscle: Resilience

Resilience is the discipline of rebuilding after disruption—integrating adversity into strength so you can rise without losing yourself in the process. It is the muscle that teaches you how to rise without rushing, repair without retreating, and return to yourself after life bends you in directions you never asked to go. If agility is the muscle that helps you pivot in motion, resilience is the one that helps you stand again when the ground beneath you moves.

In Athleadership, resilience expresses itself through **three performance capacities**, lived behaviors that determine who you become after struggle touches your life: recovery capacity, emotional bounce-back, and adaptive learning from adversity.

Recovery Capacity: Your Ability to Return to Center

Recovery capacity is the art and science of coming back to yourself after something has taken more from you than you expected to give. It's the slow reconstruction of internal equilibrium—the breath that steadies you after heartbreak, the silence that holds you after disappointment, the boundary that rebuilds you after burnout. It's not dramatic. It's deliberate. Recovery capacity is the foundation of sustainable resilience because you cannot bounce back if you never learned how.

Emotional Bounce-Back: Your Ability to Soften Without Shattering

Emotional bounce-back is the ability to feel deeply without drowning in emotions. It allows you to stay open-hearted even when life has handed you reasons to close. It's the elasticity of the soul—the knowing that emotions may surge, but they do not have to steer. Leaders often misinterpret this as "toughness," but the truth is far richer: Emotional bounce-back is tenderness with boundaries, courage with discernment, and empathy without self-abandonment.

Adaptive Learning from Adversity: Your Ability to Let Hardship Become a Teacher

Adaptive learning is the moment resilience transforms into wisdom. It's what happens when you refuse to let adversity return to you empty-handed. It's the discipline of extracting insight from what tried to break you—not out of bitterness, but out of an unshakeable belief that nothing is wasted. Adaptive learning turns pain into pattern recognition, loss into clarity, disappointment into direction. It is how leaders evolve instead of stagnating.

When these three capacities braid together, they form the architecture of true resilience—a structure strong enough to hold you when life takes an unexpected turn and soft enough to let you grow through what you never thought you'd survive. And the most surprising truth is this: Resilience is not the product of perfection, but of repair. It is built in the moments when you feel knocked down by circumstances you didn't choose, and yet somehow, you rise anyway—a little wiser, a little steadier, a little more aligned with the person you are becoming. Resilience is not about bouncing back to who you were. It is about growing into who you were meant to become.

In life, leadership, and the very places where pressure has left its fingerprints on your story, resilience is the muscle that brings you back to life—not instantly, not easily, but authentically and without pretending.

The Gap

You may not always realize when your resilience is slipping because high-performing people don't tend to fall apart dramatically; we unravel quietly. We don't collapse—we compensate. And the compensation is where the damage begins. Maybe you'll recognize yourself in one of the following descriptions.

You keep taking on "just one more thing" at work because you genuinely want to be the bridge builder, the stabilizer, the glue—but inside you're fraying. You tell yourself you can handle it, that this is what strong leaders do. But every time you absorb what the team won't address or won't confront, a small part of you absorbs the cost. And you feel it later—in irritability, fatigue, or that moment when you sit in the car after work and don't move because you need a second to become human again.

Your resilience is slipping in the form of over-functioning. Because when you can't control the outcome, you try to control the effort. You double down. You tighten your grip. You volunteer for tasks that don't belong to you or micromanage those who report to you. You replay the situation in your mind at 2:00 a.m., trying to fix something that your imagination can't fix. That's not resilience. That's survival masquerading as strength.

You stay "positive" a little too easily—smiling through disappointment, cracking a joke over heartbreak, convincing everyone (including yourself) that you're fine. But your body knows the truth. You feel the heaviness in your shoulders. The tension in your jaw. The emotional fatigue no amount of sleep seems to cure. You're not failing. You're just bypassing. And bypassing always has a bill.

You've become the person everyone comes to for support because they know you can hold things together. And you can—you always have. But you've started to notice that you don't have anyone you go to. You're carrying the weight of multiple people's worlds while silently ignoring the tremors in your own. Here's the truth: being the "strong one" is noble, but only until it becomes self-neglect.

There's the slow, quiet erosion that happens when you stay loyal to a situation long after it has stopped being loyal to your well-being. A workplace, a relationship, a responsibility, a role you've outgrown. You call it resilience, but really, it's a habit of enduring what's hurting you. The longer you stay, the more you confuse familiarity with faithfulness.

Your resilience gap shows up in busyness—the kind that looks productive but is actually avoidance dressed up in ambition. You keep moving so you don't have to feel. You keep working so you don't have to. You keep serving so you don't have to sit with the truth that something inside you is tender and tired. It's not that you don't know how to rest. It's that rest that would require honesty.

These are the quiet fractures where resilience begins to break: not in catastrophe, but in the small, daily betrayals of your own needs, your own limits, your own humanity. And if you see yourself anywhere in this—anywhere at all—hear this with compassion: What you're feeling isn't weakness; it's exhaustion. What looks like failure is often the weight you've been carrying for too long. And what feels like a lack of resilience is really resilience without space to restore. That is unsustainable for anyone.

This is why we build this muscle intentionally—not to avoid the breaking points, but to meet them with tools, truth, and practices that honor your humanity instead of depleting it.

The Science: What Resilience Really Is (And What Your Body Is Doing When You're Trying to Hold It Together)

If you've ever wondered why certain seasons stretch you thinner than others—why a small conflict unravels you or a simple request feels inexplicably heavy—the explanation is in your capacity. Long before your mind decides how strong you feel, your body has already begun negotiating the load.

Resilience is often talked about like it lives in your mindset—in grit, toughness, optimism. But in reality, resilience lives in your biology first. It's shaped by the way your nervous system absorbs stress, processes emotion, and restores balance after life hits harder than expected. It's your internal capacity to stretch without quietly tearing.

Here's the simplest truth: Your brain and body are always working to protect you—even when you interpret that protection as overwhelm.

When pressure rises, your system reacts long before you do. Yes, the amygdala plays its part, but the story doesn't end there. Your prefrontal cortex, the seat of focus and emotional regulation, begins to dim when demands pile up without recovery.[37] This is why you can be fully competent and still hit moments where you stare at your calendar, your inbox, or your child asking a simple question—and feel yourself shut down. That shutdown isn't weakness; it's neural depletion. Another system—your anterior cingulate cortex—helps you stay steady through conflict. When you've stretched too long, this area loses bandwidth, which is why a tone shift in a meeting or an unexpected request can feel sharper, heavier, or more personal than it should.[38] Your insula, which monitors your internal cues, becomes more active under strain. This is why your breath shortens, your chest tightens, or your stomach drops even when you tell yourself, *I'm fine.* Your body reports truth faster than your words.

And the HPA axis—your internal stress engine—determines how much fuel you have left. When overactivated, it begins firing cortisol at the wrong moments. You find yourself reactive when the moment is small, numb when the moment is meaningful, and confused by your own emotional swings.

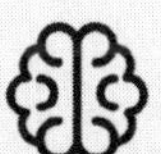

This is all part of allostatic load—the cost of being strong for too long without repair. Every time you push through exhaustion, silence disappointment, or say "I'll handle it" when you're already stretched thin, your resilience account takes a withdrawal. Withdrawals without deposits don't make you stronger. They make you brittle.

That's why resilience is about smart recovery rather than endurance. Coming back to your MVP—your mission, vision, and purpose—is your compass to keep moving forward, even when you are relying on resilience most. Think of a challenging time that you may be facing that brings stress and uncertainty. Having a vision and belief that things will get better can become a lifeline. It speeds up the process of your inner world returning to center after being stretched. It gives your nervous system the flexibility to come back online after disruption. It allows you to quietly return to yourself after you've been pulled in a hundred directions.

You can look strong on the outside and still be unraveling inside. Your biology often tells the truth first. Resilience is not proven by how much you carry, but by how you come back.

Once you realize your body is not betraying you but protecting you, you stop judging yourself for feeling depleted. You start listening, repairing, and building resilience the right way: not through force, but through restoration. Because resilience isn't the art of pushing through. It's the practice of coming back home to yourself over and over again.

You weren't meant to carry all this weight with willpower alone. Your MVP is the anchor that reminds you *why* you rise again, not just *how*.

Athlete in Action:
Alex Smith, Retired NFL Quarterback

There are comeback stories, and then there is the story of Alex Smith—the kind that forces you to slow down and reconsider what resilience truly requires. When his leg shattered in 2018, it wasn't the kind of injury athletes tape up and push through. It was catastrophic. The kind that makes most people look away. The kind that threatens not only a career but a life.

What most didn't see was what happened after the stadium lights dimmed: 17 surgeries, a life-threatening flesh-eating infection, months of immobilization, and the delicate, uncertain work of teaching a leg—and a spirit—how to bear weight again. Doctors weren't trying to restore a quarterback. They were trying to save a life.

He later admitted, with an honesty that stopped me the first time I heard it, "I was scared to death." Scared the bone would break again. Scared the doctors were wrong. Scared he would become a public spectacle of failure. Scared that trusting his body again was asking too much.

This is the part of resilience leaders rarely acknowledge: Fear lingers long after the crisis has passed.

Smith didn't erase that fear. He simply refused to let it drive. Resilience for him was not a roar but a returning to discipline, to presence, to inner truth. It was the slow rebuilding of trust: in his leg, in his instincts, in his future. It was walking step-by-step toward the very arena that once almost destroyed him. Two years later, when he jogged onto that football field, it wasn't triumph that defined the moment. It was surrender—to the work he had done, to the risk he was willing to shoulder, and to the belief that purpose is worth stepping back into the unknown for.

His comeback wasn't miraculous or flashy. It was methodical, faithful, about becoming someone stronger. Resilience isn't overcoming once. It's choosing to keep becoming—especially when fear whispers that you shouldn't try again. Alex Smith reminds us that true resilience is not measured by speed, bravado, or applause. It's measured by the courage to trust yourself in the very place you were once broken.

Athleader in Action
Mary Barra, CEO, General Motors

There is a chapter of Mary Barra's story that most people gloss over because it is uncomfortable—not scandalous, but deeply human in the way that only true leadership moments are. When people talk about her rise at General Motors, they highlight her being the first woman to lead a major automaker, her engineering background, and her operational brilliance. What they often forget is the moment she stepped into the CEO role—and the storm waiting for her there. Barra didn't inherit a throne. She inherited a crisis.

Only weeks into her new role as CEO in 2013, she was handed a recall tragedy involving faulty ignition switches linked to multiple deaths. It was a crisis born years before she sat in the seat, yet she became the face of its accountability. Most leaders would have instinctively distanced themselves, softened their tone, or tried to control the narrative. But Barra did something different—something we rarely see in corporate life and almost never witness at that scale. She stepped toward the fire.

Not with spin or platitudes, but with the sober clarity of someone who understood that leadership is not about timing; it is about truth-telling. She looked grieving families in the eye. She sat with their stories. She listened to pain she didn't cause but chose to carry. When she testified before Congress, she didn't hide behind legal counsel or corporate armor. She told the truth—even when it was heavy, even when it exposed the depth of GM's internal failures, even when the world waited to judge her next sentence. That's resilience. Not the grit of pushing through, but the courage of staying present inside a moment most leaders would emotionally evacuate.

And if you look carefully, you can see the deeper lesson—the one that speaks directly to every high-performing leader who feels the weight of expectations, complexity, and inherited challenges.

Barra wasn't just managing a crisis. She was absorbing the anger without letting it calcify into defensiveness. She was holding the institutional shame without letting it distort her identity. She was meeting the suffering of others without collapsing under the guilt of it. That is advanced emotional resilience—the kind that doesn't simply bounce back but *grows back*, stronger, cleaner, and more grounded in purpose.

Out of that crucible came something only a resilient leader can embody: a mandate to rebuild trust not as a PR exercise, but as a cultural reformation. She made sweeping changes to GM's internal processes. She tore down silos. She reshaped accountability. She rebuilt the company's safety practices from the inside out. And quietly, behind the headlines, she became a model of what it means to lead with moral clarity when the path in front of you was paved by someone else's neglect.

The world praises her now for electric vehicle innovation, strategic clarity, and long-term transformation. But I believe her true leadership—the part that touches the human heart—was forged in those early months, when she had to confront a truth many leaders would choose to avoid. Sometimes resilience isn't about being strong. Sometimes it's about refusing to turn away.

For every leader reading this who is carrying something you didn't choose—a broken system you inherited, a team culture you didn't create, a family crisis that arrived uninvited, a responsibility that feels too heavy for one pair of hands—Barra's story is your reminder: You can walk into a fire you didn't start and still become the leader who transforms it.

Resilience isn't what happens after the crisis. It is who you become inside the crisis.

The Reflection

What stays with me about Barra and Smith is not the scale of their roles or the visibility of their platforms, but the way their stories reveal the truth that resilience is never reserved for the extraordinary. It is forged in the same human places where you and I have stood, breath held, heart trembling, wondering how we are going to make it through a moment that did not care about our plans, our timelines, or our carefully managed expectations. Their experiences simply magnify something you've already lived in your own way: the slow, private negotiations we make with ourselves when life shifts beneath us without notice, asking more of us than we believed we had to give.

Because if you strip away the titles, the stadium lights, the boardrooms, and the global headlines, what remains in both of their stories is something deeply familiar—that quiet, unspoken moment when you realize the life you were living has been interrupted, not by choice but by force, and now you must decide whether you will allow the disruption to define you or whether you will stay long enough inside the wound for it to become a well of strength you didn't know you possessed. This is a moment every person, in every walk of life, knows intimately: the teacher who still shows up to her classroom while navigating the ache of a dissolving marriage; the father who carries the weight of providing while silently battling a fear he cannot name; the young professional who sits in her car before walking into a job that drains her spirit, whispering a prayer for the strength to make it through one more day; the woman who wakes up after loss and has to renegotiate her identity with the pieces that remain.

Resilience is not something that happens far above us—it happens within us, often quietly, often invisibly, often without applause. These are the unsung arenas of resilience—no medals, no headlines, no leadership awards, just you and the quiet decision not to give up on yourself.

Even the strongest among us can carry so much for so long that we forget what our own weight feels like. You push through because the moment demands it. You keep going because someone has to. You hold everything together because you learned early that collapse was not an option. Yet underneath that strength, there may be a part of you whispering truths you've been too busy—or too loyal—to hear. The fatigue that doesn't disappear with sleep. The frustration you swallow because you don't want to add your pain to the pile. The tenderness you hide because vulnerability feels like a luxury you're not sure you can afford. The hush of your own unmet needs. This, too, is part of resilience—the cost of being the one others depend on.

Ask yourself: Where in your life have you mistaken endurance for healing? Where are you surviving what you were never meant to survive alone? Where have you quieted your own ache in the name of being "strong"? These questions aren't accusations—they are invitations to see yourself with the same compassion you extend so easily to others and to recognize that resilience is not measured by how much you can tolerate, but by how honestly you can tell the truth about what your journey has required of you.

Barra rebuilt a company through truth-telling. Smith rebuilt a body through surrender. You are rebuilding something, too—even if the world doesn't yet see the scaffolding. This is where your resilience begins—not in the push, but in the pause long enough to honor the story you're living.

1. What pressure point in my life is asking for recovery, not pushing?
2. Where am I breaking my own boundaries in the name of being strong?
3. What is one habit I can rebuild this week that restores my strength?

The Conditioning:
The Reset Drill for Resilience

You don't need a brand-new set of tools for every Core 4 muscle. Conditioning is about continuity with elevation—a system that becomes deeper, sharper, and more transformative as you build mental muscle memory. Agility explored how to reset in a moment. Resilience will now show you how to reset in a season. A signature, system-wide drill for Athleadership, the Reset helps restore executive function under pressure. It's designed to interrupt the hijacking of your mind, so you can choose the next step. Use this drill any time you feel emotionally stretched, mentally depleted, spiritually tired, or internally unraveling. It's the smallest, most essential form of conditioning.

5 Words → 2 Truths → 1 Choice

Here's how it works:

STEP ❶: **5 Words**	Say (out loud or silently): **"I bend—I don't break."** These five words calm the fear of collapse. Reignite belief in your capacity to endure. You can find your own or select from any of these three: "I'm allowed to feel—still rising." "This is heavy—I'm here." "Hard moment—stronger me emerging."
STEP ❷: **2 Truths**	Instead of two options in agility, resilience asks for two truths you must face: What is the pain or pressure I'm actually feeling? What strength is still available to me right now? This keeps resilience from becoming emotional avoidance. It merges honesty and hope to form the inner scaffolding that endurance rests on.
STEP ❸: **1 Choice**	Choose one small act of forward motion in the next 24 hours. Resilience works slowly because courage takes time. The outcome is that we hope for emotional fortitude. It could be something simple, such as get out of bed, call a friend, write a paragraph in my journal, take a walk, pray when you don't know what to say, cook a meal, say no to something that drains you, choose rest without apology. The size doesn't matter; the movement does.

How to Apply the Drill: My Story of Resilience

Let's come back to my journey through loss and purpose and use it as an example to see how this works inside resilience.

5 Words: "I bend—I don't break."

When grief washed over me in my early-twenties, I dealt with sudden loss that shattered me. These are the five words that grounded my emotional truth: "This won't take me out." (Remember, you can choose your own or use the examples I shared.)

2 Truths

"I am hurting. I am carrying disappointment."

"I am still becoming. There is purpose in my pain."

This part of the drill names the pain and names the strength, so the nervous system has something to hold onto.

1 Choice (24-hour window)

"Focus on someone else."

For me, that choice eventually became purpose—the birth of Velvet Suite, the beginning of discovering my why, the decision to prepare space for the love I believed would someday return. And when that love finally arrived—quickly, beautifully, unexpectedly—it met a woman who had already rebuilt her inner world with intention. However, there were really sad, lonely, and frustrating days. I didn't want to get up or do anything. In those moments, I would give myself space to honor what I was authentically feeling. Then, I made a commitment to reach out to one person and do something for someone else. This was how I would move forward, a simple step-by-step. I'd make a phone call, send a text, give a compliment. Anything to turn my pain into purpose for others.

The Practice: Your Resilience Reset in Activation

Use this in real time, in any moment when life hits harder than you were ready for.

Say your five words.

"I bend—I don't break." (*Drill*)

Speak your two truths—one about your pain, one about your strength. (*Reps*)

Take one small step in the next 24 hours to honor your humanity and affirm your future. (*Rhythm*)

Give yourself space—an evening off, a reset weekend, a walk without your phone. Resilience needs room to breathe. (*Recovery*)

Ask: "What did this moment teach me about who I am becoming?" This is how resilience becomes identity, not reaction.

The Integration: Where Resilience Becomes Rebirth

Resilience is never built in the spotlight; it's shaped in the quiet, unseen places where life confronts you with what you did not choose and asks, *What will you do now?* It is the muscle that lets you breathe after the blow, rise after unraveling, and trust after disappointment rearranges the map you were following. And if this chapter has shown you anything, I hope it's this: You are allowed to be remade without being diminished.

Resilience is not bouncing back to who you were; it's growing forward into who you're becoming—without losing yourself in the process. It is not the art of bouncing back quickly; it is the discipline of rising honestly. It's the long obedience of healing, the willingness to tell the truth about what hurts, and the courage to rebuild without bitterness. It refuses the lie that you have to pretend everything is fine and instead teaches you how to stand—shaking if you must—inside a life you are still learning how to carry.

And the experiences that once threatened to break you? They do not become monuments that define you. They become milestones—markers of passage, proof that you walked through what others thought would destroy you and found a deeper identity on the other side. Resilience reshapes the story you tell about your past, not by erasing the pain, but by refusing to let it hold the pen.

When resilience strengthens, your entire internal architecture shifts: Agility becomes quicker, alignment becomes clearer, and well-being stops being something you practice and becomes something you protect. You begin to recognize that your power was never in avoiding pressure, but in becoming someone who does not disappear when pressure arrives. One stabilizes you in motion; the other rebuilds you after impact—and together they form the first two pillars of sustainable leadership maturity. And at the center of every resilient comeback is your MVP—the compass that steadies your steps when the path ahead is still rebuilding beneath you.

Once resilience is rooted in you, you are ready to build the next muscle with deeper clarity, cleaner purpose, and more internal strength than before. Alignment is waiting—and it will ask for everything resilience has prepared you to give.

9

Alignment: Purpose-Driven Performance

*"Building a visionary company requires
one percent vision and 99 percent alignment."*

—Jim Collins and Jerry Porras, *Built to Last*

There are seasons in leadership when the work you are doing is undeniably good, impactful, and purpose-filled—and yet, if you're honest, something in you knows it is no longer the full truth of who you are becoming. I found myself in one of those seasons not long ago. The She-Suite, a female-focused platform under Velvet Suite, had been a vibrant expression of my purpose for over a decade—a movement that lifted women, amplified voices, and created space where there once was none. It was, and will always be, part of my DNA. Alignment, I've learned, is not a shrine you build once; it is a living, breathing conversation between who you are and who you are becoming, season by season. And somewhere in the quiet corners of my life, I felt that conversation shifting.

I didn't recognize it at first, but I could sense the exhaustion, the friction, the subtle ache of doing work that was meaningful, yet no longer the whole assignment. I felt the tension between the impact we were making and the impact I knew was still possible. And if I'm honest, I could feel the weight of what people expected from me—a version of my purpose that was familiar, celebrated, proven. But alignment will always ask you to choose truth over applause. And the truth was this: We were changing lives, but we were not yet changing leadership at the scale the moment demanded.

Clarity came when I least expected it—during my recovery from a major surgery, when stillness became my mandatory teacher. My husband, Will, and I would meet on Fridays for a gentle walk, the kind where your body is healing but your heart is listening. Without planning to, I said aloud what my heart had been whispering for years: "There is a model I've been carrying my whole life—a secret strategy I've watched in athletes, executives, and inside my own story. And I don't see this mental model accessible to the world." As soon as the words left my mouth, something inside me clicked back into place—not a moment of ambition but a moment of remembrance—a moment where purpose recognizes itself.

In that moment, I realized something almost sacred: The athletic lens had been guiding me long before I ever named it. It was embedded in my own mission, vision, and purpose (MVP), stitched into the frameworks I built for the She-Suite, the Band Leadership Institute, the NFL, and every enterprise leader our ed-tech platform and content had ever coached. For nearly 20 years, I had been teaching the rhythm, rigor, and mental conditioning of this mindset without ever calling it what it was. Athleadership wasn't a reinvention; it was a homecoming.

I realized the mindset I had been using my whole life—the athlete mindset, quietly—had shaped every breakthrough I'd ever had. My career and my body grew stronger because of my mind. It was the source of my endurance through illness and the stability that carried me through loss. It was the courage that helped me pivot Summit 2020 in real time, and the fuel that kept a company alive for over 20 years in a world that shifts beneath your feet without apology. My true identity had always been an Athleader. It just took alignment for me to call it by its name.

And yet, naming it wasn't the hard part. The hard part was acknowledging the misalignment I had learned to tolerate: the frustration of doing meaningful work but missing the deeper impact I was created to make; the fatigue of working hard instead of working aligned; the grace to realize that I was living my way into the answers that could only be realized through the life experiences that met the moment my leadership was needed, in the here and now. The She-Suite is still a powerful part of our arsenal, but if we were going to redefine leadership—not just for women, but for everyone—we had to address the root issue quietly crippling leaders across the world: mindset as the new skillset.

That walk revealed something I could no longer unsee. Leaders were stuck—not because they lacked talent, education, or opportunity, but because change was outpacing their capacity to adapt. I had spent more than 18 months interviewing over 1,500 executives across industries and continents, and the pattern was unmistakable: brilliant people frozen in indecision, exhausted by pressure, overwhelmed by expectations, and unprepared for the uncertainty shaping the modern workplace. They didn't need more content. They needed a new operating system—a way to transition from holding a leadership title to actually becoming the kind of leader the moment required.

This was alignment, not a pivot or a rebrand. It was a return, a remembrance, a reclamation of the mindset that built my life and could now build a new standard for leaders everywhere.

Alignment is never permanent. It is a continual return to what is true in the season you are living. It is the willingness to let go of who you were—even the successful, celebrated, beloved versions of you—to become who your purpose is calling forward now. It is the courage to ask: *What needs to evolve? What needs to be released? What is waiting to emerge?*

Peace followed. Joy followed. Freedom followed. Alignment will always unlock what effort alone cannot. It is the moment the internal gears click back into place and your life and relationships finally match the truth of your purpose.

Alignment is the only way forward. Without it, Athleadership cannot exist. With it, everything you are called to becomes possible. And once I recognized that alignment is not a one-time decision but a continual returning, it became clear that the muscle we build next is the one that keeps every leader grounded when everything else begins to pull them off course.

The Premise

Before we dive into alignment, I want to bring you back to the truth at the center of this entire journey: Pressure doesn't just test your capacity—it tests your coherence. Every leader can move fast. Far fewer move in the right direction.

Alignment is the Core 4 muscle that holds you steady when everything around you is trying to pull you out of position. It is the discipline to stay connected to who you are, what you value, and what you're called to do, even when circumstances tempt you to abandon your center. Most leaders drift not because they don't care, but because urgency becomes louder than purpose. Expectations—from others, from culture, from your own internal critic—begin to drag you into decisions that look productive but quietly fracture your integrity, your priorities, your relationships, and your energy. You end up living by reaction instead of conviction, performing roles instead of embodying your purpose, and managing fires instead of building a future.

In moments of change, you may cling to the familiar and comfortable and miss what change requires of you now. Here's the truth most leaders never pause long enough to realize: The world around you isn't what derails you. It's the way you assess the distance between your values and your choices that does.

Alignment isn't about perfection. It's about coherence—the internal unity that allows your mind, your mission, and your movement to operate as one. When you are aligned, your decisions become cleaner, your priorities sharpen, and your team feels your consistency. Your presence becomes more grounding. And pressure stops scattering you and starts sharpening you.

Because everything you build—your leadership, your purpose, your influence, your relationships—rests on the stability of who you are when pressure hits.

Alignment is the muscle that gathers all the scattered parts of you and brings them back into a coherent whole. It is the quiet, internal recalibration that happens when you realize the life you are leading and the life you are called to live have begun drifting apart. That drift is rarely dramatic. It often begins with good intentions, a "yes" meant to help someone else, a compromise meant to keep the peace, a role you step into because you can but never stop to ask whether you should. Over time, these small departures from yourself accumulate. The inches between your life and your purpose widen, and before you can describe what is happening, your speed increases and carries you away from the MVP that centers you. Alignment is the discipline that interrupts that drift and gently—sometimes urgently—guides you back home.

It asks a more demanding question than "What now?" It asks, "From where within me am I moving?" Alignment is not a posture you achieve once; it is a rhythm you practice continually—a cadence of realignment, reassessment, and renewed conviction. **It requires a leader to stand** honestly in the mirror and tell the truth about what is driving their decisions: purpose or pressure, clarity or confusion, calling or conditioning. When this muscle is strong, your movements have an internal integrity. You are no longer performing leadership—you are embodying it.

Alignment is also a spiritual state, an interior congruence that strengthens you from the inside out. When you are aligned, you stop living as a fragmented version of yourself, pulled in pieces by obligation, ambition, and expectation. You begin living as one integrated being. Your mission speaks louder than noise. Your priorities stop contradicting your values. And your decisions, even the hard ones, begin to feel like truth rather than negotiation.

This is why alignment is one of the most essential muscles in the Core 4. Without it, agility turns into frantic motion, resilience turns into survival, and well-being turns into repair instead of renewal. Alignment steadies the system—spiritually, mentally, emotionally—and anchors your MVP so your path is not determined by circumstance but by calling. It is the muscle that ensures the life you are building is actually the life you were meant to live.

The Muscle: Alignment

Alignment is purpose in motion, a continual returning. It is the internal recalibration that helps you remain connected to who you are and what you value, even as the world around you accelerates and pulls you in competing directions. In modern leadership, where urgency often overshadows intention, alignment becomes the stabilizing force that ensures your movement still matches your meaning.

At its core, alignment expresses itself through **three behavioral dimensions** that determine how coherently you show up in life and leadership. It begins with goal clarity and prioritization, the ability to filter noise, establish what matters most, and arrange your decisions around those priorities. When this dimension weakens, leaders drift—succeeding at work that looks impressive but quietly misdirects their energy. When it strengthens, your efforts begin to compound with precision rather than scatter through obligation.

In communication, alignment is the consistency between your words, your expectations, and your actual behavior. Many leaders articulate clarity but operate in contradiction—encouraging boundaries they do not model, promising focus without protecting it, communicating vision while living in urgency. When communication aligns, your presence becomes a signal of steadiness, and people learn to trust not just what you say, but how you live it.

Finally, alignment is reinforced through collaboration agility, your ability to work with others in ways that honor both direction and partnership. Misalignment here often hides behind competence: You contribute, you deliver, you collaborate, but the environments or relationships no longer match the direction you are growing in. When collaboration is aligned, you surround yourself with people, rhythms, and partnerships that strengthen who you are becoming rather than anchor you to who you were.

Together, these dimensions form the architecture of aligned performance. When this muscle is weak, leaders don't fall apart—they drift. They operate with high capability but low clarity. They execute tasks that look strategic but feel hollow. They live in a kind of quiet tension where effort rises while fulfillment fades. Alignment rarely breaks loudly; it dissolves quietly.

When alignment is strong, your leadership sharpens. Decisions become cleaner. Priorities become simpler. Your presence becomes more grounding. You stop performing roles and start leading from a centered, congruent place. Alignment turns pressure into focus, noise into clarity, and constant motion into meaningful progress.

This muscle keeps you honest. It ensures agility doesn't devolve into frantic pivoting, and resilience doesn't become survival mode. Alignment brings the system back into coherence so your leadership moves in the same direction as your purpose.

This is the muscle we strengthen now.

The Gap: When Your Life Looks Full but Feels Off-Center

Misalignment rarely announces itself with exhaustion or collapse; that belongs to other muscles. Alignment slips through far quieter doors. It shows up when your life is *working*, but something essential is no longer *true*.

It's the subtle dissonance you feel when your calendar is full of good work that is no longer your work. The heaviness of carrying a role that stopped fitting you months ago.

The quiet ache of realizing you've become indispensable in places that no longer feel aligned with where you're growing.

Alignment breaks first in the place where your inner "yes" becomes a polite "I guess." You tell yourself you're being a team player. You rationalize: "This is what leaders do." You lean into duty instead of conviction. You move from intention to inertia. And slowly, without noticing, you begin living a life that is externally impressive and directionally inaccurate.

The gap widens when you keep succeeding at things you no longer feel called to. The world applauds, but your inner world grows strangely quiet. You say yes to opportunities that elevate your visibility but dilute your purpose. You're seen more widely but known less truly. You start making decisions based on who might be disappointed, not who you're becoming. It is people-pleasing disguised as professionalism.

This is the unique ache of alignment drift: Nothing is falling apart, but nothing feels fully alive either. Drifting is dangerous because it looks like high-functioning leadership—until suddenly it doesn't. The misalignment becomes noticeable in moments you can't easily explain— the meeting where you speak but don't recognize your own voice, the achievement that lands with silence instead of joy, or the opportunity that checks every strategic box but leaves your spirit unmoved.

You begin to sense it in the gap between the leader you've become and the leader you're becoming. There is friction between what is working and what you want. Alignment doesn't slip because you failed, but because you stopped listening.

The Science: Why Alignment Works

Alignment is emotional, intuitive, and deeply neurobiological. When you are aligned, the brain shifts from fragmentation to integration. Research shows that coherence between values, goals, and behavior activates the medial prefrontal cortex, the region responsible for identity, decision-making, and long-term planning.[39] This is the executive center of the brain that allows leaders to make choices rooted in purpose, not panic. Misalignment, on the other hand, triggers chronic cognitive dissonance—the draining, invisible tension between what you believe and what you do. Neuroscientists describe this sustained strain as a psychophysiological cost,[40] and leaders pay it with exhaustion, irritability, and impaired judgment. When your actions and your values move in different directions, the brain must work double-time to maintain the performance of stability—a cost that eventually shows up as burnout, disengagement, or emotional collapse.

Alignment also strengthens what psychologists call self-congruence, a state associated with resilience, fulfillment, and high performance. When leaders operate from congruence, the anterior cingulate cortex—the brain's conflict-monitoring system—quiets, allowing for smoother decision-making and reduced emotional volatility. Your mind and body register alignment as safety, stability, and ease. Alignment also increases access to flow states—those periods of deep focus and fluid productivity where time stretches and creativity sharpens. Flow requires neurological harmony: clarity of intention, reduction of noise, and coherence of goals. And when you integrate alignment with agility and resilience, your brain is no longer simply managing change—it is metabolizing it, using pressure as the catalyst for clarity.

Athlete in Action:
Olympic Gold Medal Swimmer, Michael Phelps

There is a moment in Michael Phelps's story that most people rush past because it is quieter than a podium, darker than a victory lap, and harder to celebrate. It happened after the medals—after the world crowned him the greatest Olympian in history, after the final roar of the crowd had dissolved into memory. Most people assume that alignment is only a question for those who are struggling, wandering, or searching for direction. Sometimes the greatest misalignment arrives not when life is falling apart, but when everything you worked for has finally come true.

For Phelps, that moment came in the silence after triumph. He had spent years forging a life inside the water, his body conditioned to rise before dawn, his mind calibrated to endure the grueling monotony of training, his identity tethered to performance. He was celebrated, decorated, and adored. But beneath the surface, something quieter and far more dangerous was unfolding: He had achieved the pinnacle of success without the scaffolding of alignment to support it.

When the final race was over and the lane lines stilled, Michael stepped out of the pool and realized that everything he had built had been structured around a single identity: swimmer. The problem was not that the identity was false; it was that the identity was incomplete. And incomplete identities collapse under the weight of expectation.

What followed was a descent so steep that even he struggled to recognize himself. He faced depression, addiction, self-destruction, and the terrifying honesty that he no longer wanted to live. These were not the signs of someone weak—they were the symptoms of someone wildly out of alignment with his core. His purpose, his values, his emotional truth, his own humanity had been sacrificed at the altar of achievement. And when the applause stopped, the misalignment remained.

Phelps didn't find alignment in another medal or another training cycle. He found it in stillness. In therapy. In finally telling the truth—to himself first, and then to the world. He found it in the faces of the people who loved him, not for what he won, but for who he was fighting to become. He found it in the realization that performance cannot be purpose, and achievement cannot be identity.

His alignment began the moment he finally asked the question he had never been given permission to ask: Who am I without the water?

What emerged was not a comeback story, but a coherence story—one where Michael began rebuilding his life from the inside out. He anchored himself in mental health advocacy. He learned how to be present as a husband and father. He shifted from chasing greatness to stewarding it. The man who had once lived in relentless pursuit became a man who lived in intentional alignment—purpose-led, heart-aware, spiritually grounded, and emotionally honest.

Phelps's medals remained extraordinary, but they were no longer the measure of who he was as a human. And in that redefinition, his impact expanded beyond the pool, beyond the Olympics, beyond the metrics that once defined him. He became an advocate for millions, a voice for mental health, a model for leaders who look successful on paper but feel fractured in private.

Michael Phelps's story teaches us something essential about alignment that no trophy ever could: You can win everything the world celebrates and still lose yourself. But when you return to what matters—your truth, your values, your calling—your life becomes coherent, your leadership becomes whole, and your impact becomes infinitely larger than your achievements. Alignment in motion isn't perfection or performance; it's returning to the deepest truth of who you are, and choosing to live from there.

Athleader in Action:
Satya Nadella, CEO, Microsoft

There are moments in a leader's life when alignment does not arrive as clarity, but as a break—a quiet, profound unraveling of what you thought leadership required. For Satya Nadella, that moment came the day his son, Zain, was born. Zain was born with severe cerebral palsy, which would bring a lifetime of medical dependency and a world that didn't match the one Satya had imagined for his family. His first instinct might have been the same reflex many high achievers don't admit aloud: *Why us? Why me? How will this impact my life?* But as he watched his wife, Anu, bend toward their son with a fierce and tender devotion, something in him shifted. What he witnessed was not despair; it was a radical reorientation, a turning of the heart aligned, a different kind of strength.

Zain's life became a lens that clarified everything Nadella had missed in the earlier version of himself. He learned—slowly, and with a humility that reshapes a soul—that leadership was not merely the exercise of intellect or execution, but the discipline of seeing others deeply. He began to understand that alignment is not an internal monologue; it is an external responsibility. It is meeting the world through someone else's limitations, someone else's pain, someone else's possibility. Compassion became his apprenticeship into a different kind of power that places the leader among the people instead of above them.

When he stepped into the CEO role at Microsoft in 2014, he shaped a new mission for himself and the company—*"to empower every person and every organization on the planet to achieve more."* It was alignment, born with the boy who depended on accessible tech to survive and from the father who understood what it meant to navigate a world not built with everybody in mind. Zain was not a footnote to Nadella's leadership; he was the reason it matured into what the world now recognizes as an empathetic, expansive, and human-centered corporate transformation story.

When Zain passed away in 2022 at the age of 26, Nadella's alignment did not fracture. Loss sharpened what purpose had already revealed: that leadership is not the optimization of performance but the orchestration of meaning. It is returning, again and again, to what matters most—even when the terrain of your life has been irrevocably altered. Nadella's story reminds us that alignment is not a fixed state, but a living practice. It is a willingness to let your deepest truth reshape how you lead, how you listen, how you build, and how you serve. His alignment did not come through success; it came through surrender, grief, and love. It emerged through the radical humility of asking not, "How does this affect me?" but "What does this moment require of me?"

The Reflection

Alignment always reveals itself in the same quiet truth. There comes a moment when who you have been and who you are becoming can no longer live in the same space. Michael Phelps felt it in the silence after the greatest victories of his life, when achievement could no longer hold the weight of identity. Satya Nadella felt it in the hospital room with his son, when leadership stopped being about strategy and became an act of deep, human empathy.

Alignment begins the moment you stop performing the role the world applauds and return to the truth that is asking to lead you forward. It demands the courage to let your internal *yes* become louder than the expectations around you. And when you honor that shift— even in small ways—your life begins to move with a coherence you can feel, and others can follow.

▷◁ ALIGNMENT PULSE CHECK-IN

1. What part of my leadership feels "off" even though it looks successful?
2. Where am I saying yes out of obligation instead of conviction?
3. What is one choice I can make today that returns me to what matters now?

The Conditioning:
The Reset Drill for Alignment

This is the signature, system-wide drill for Athleadership. It helps restore executive function under pressure. It's designed to interrupt the hijacking of your mind when choosing the next step.

5 Words → 2 Truths → 1 Promise

Here's how it works:

STEP ❶:
5 Words

Say (out loud or silently): **"Return to what matters now."**

This is your internal cue, the sentence that interrupts drift before a drift becomes a detour. These five words are not meant to inspire you—they are meant to regulate you. They tell your brain: *Come back home.*

You can find your own or select from any of these:

"I choose purpose over posture."
"I choose alignment over fear."
"Return to my core values."

When I said to myself, "I choose alignment over fear," something in my nervous system settled. The striving quieted, the urgency softened, and my brain could finally access clarity because I had stopped to listen.

STEP ❷:
2 Truths

What is real and what is required? Alignment is not about choosing between options; it's about facing truths. Two truths, specifically:

- What is true about where I am?
- What is true about what this season is asking of me?

For me, the truths were simple and seismic:

- *I am making an impact . . . and there are pieces of my purpose dormant.*
- *I have been leading women . . . and I am called to lead every leader navigating change.*

Truth creates clean lines inside the mind. It wipes away the fog.

Set aside the whole strategy and your whole figure, and instead choose one aligned move that matches your MVP. For me, that move was listening and interviewing 1,500 leaders, sitting in their pain and gathering their patterns. Naming the real problem under the surface: *People are not prepared to lead through the pressure and pace of change.*

STEP ❸:
1 Promise

One aligned step gave me clarity, which created courage, which became Athleadership. I didn't feel the change overnight, but after continuing to come back home, time and time again, I could see the positive impact on my life and mindset. It gave me the motivation to keep choosing these reset drills through the pressure and pace of leading through change.

Alignment is built through the daily, disciplined return to your true self.

The Everyday Example

Alignment isn't only found on healing walks or major life pivots; it also lives in the hallway moments of our work and life. Imagine you're a leader carrying a team through a reorganization. Your calendar stays full. Everyone needs you. You're praised for being steady under pressure. But privately, you feel the drift. You're doing good work, but it's not your work. You're performing competence instead of living conviction. You're saying yes to everything because you don't want to disappoint anyone, but your values are slipping out of the frame.

Here's what alignment looks like in that ordinary, sacred moment: You step away from your screen and whisper your five words, "Return to what matters now." Your heartbeat settles. Your mind clears just enough to access honesty.

Then the two truths come forward:

- *I am capable, but I am depleted.*
- *This season requires clarity, not more effort.*

From there, your one default becomes clear: *Cancel the meeting that doesn't need you. Call the one that does. Say no to the project that pulls you away from alignment. Say yes to the one that protects it.*

One aligned step rewrites the day. Step-by-step, you rewrite your life.

The Practice: Your Alignment Activation

Here's how you embody alignment in real time, refined for this muscle:

Pause + Return (*Drill*)

Say your five words slowly enough that your body can believe them: "Return to what matters now."

Name Two Truths (*Rep*)

- What is true about where you are?
- What is true about what this season needs?

Choose One Promise (*Rhythm*)

Pick one step that reflects your values—not your fears.

Restore Before Acting (*Recovery*)

Take three slow breaths, let your nervous system settle, then make the move.

This is not a checklist. This is the essential check-in to ensure you are on target, on task, and on time for what matters most in this season of your leadership.

The Integration

Alignment is the Core 4 muscle that makes every other muscle honest. It gathers the clarity of agility and the strength of resilience and points them toward purpose. Without alignment, beautiful effort becomes misplaced and leaders drift into roles that look impressive but drain their lives of meaning. But with alignment—the quiet, disciplined return to what matters—your leadership stops scattering and starts shaping.

When you integrate the Alignment Drill into your lived rhythm, something powerful happens. You stop abandoning yourself in the name of achievement. You begin to honor the truth within you at the speed life demands of you. You become a leader who moves from conviction, not reaction; from purpose, not pressure.

This is where the Athleader begins to take full form—a leader who doesn't just perform excellence, but embodies coherence. A leader built for the moment and self-aware to maximize their greatest gifts for what the world needs in that moment.

10

Well-Being: Sustain Your Energy

"It's not the load that breaks you down, it's the way you carry it."

—Lou Holtz, Football coach and television analyst

Sometimes we don't realize how easy it is to drift away from the reason you work until joy touches you again and something inside you remembers. For me, that reminder didn't arrive in a crisis or a collapse. It came quietly, during an ordinary dinner, barefoot in the kitchen, sitting at the kiddie table while my son, Kingston, laughed—one of those bright, unfiltered, little-boy laughs that ripples through a home and resets the air. I didn't just hear him. I felt him. I felt myself—present, unhurried, alive in a way I hadn't been in a while. And it startled me, the way joy can arrive like a reunion with a part of you that had been waiting.

I realized I had built this business with the intention of creating more space and flexibility. But without clear and consistent boundaries, I would be living adjacent to my own life—close enough to function, far enough to forget how it felt to inhabit joy fully.

163

My career has taught me grit, fulfillment, and endurance. Connecting with my purpose had taught me intention and impact. But motherhood taught me the absolute joy of being present. It revealed the truth that no accomplishment, no platform, no title would ever matter more than being well enough—body, mind, and spirit—to show up for the moments that matter. I didn't want my son to inherit my pain as normal. I wanted him to inherit my joy and capacity to savor and to be fully present.

My Breaking Became My Beginning

The recovery from the major surgery I mentioned earlier pulled me into mandatory stillness. Recovery forced me to confront the cost of a life lived on adrenaline. I could no longer outrun what my body had been whispering for years: *You matter, too.* This time, I didn't want to climb back into the same patterns. I wanted to come back home—to myself, to God, to a way of living that was sustainable, joyful, and honest. My theme song, "Enjoy" by Janet Jackson, played on repeat in my earphones as I gained strength to walk, jog, and eventually run again. I made room to dance, laugh, and enjoy!

My well-being in my recovery became my top priority. I reached out for accountability and support on my journey. My coach, Ryall, stepped into my story with a kind of fierce gentleness. She held up a mirror, not to what I had accomplished, but to who I really was as an Athleader. She held me accountable for restoring my vitality, my rest, and my passion for fitness. I built practices that weren't glamorous or grand, but grounding—returning me to a rhythm that I had lost touch with in the hustle of life. Breath by breath and rep by rep, well-being became a doorway into a life I could feel. The transformation wasn't quick, but it was true: I lost 50 pounds, yes—but more importantly, I shed the weight of years of emotional strain. I reclaimed my athletic edge—not in pursuit of an image, but in service of my Athleader identity. I rediscovered a joy I had forgotten I deserved. And the most precious part of it all? I became a more present mother, a more grounded wife, and a more whole leader.

Well-being isn't accomplished once. It is a daily practice, a never-ending journey. Some days you soar, and others you stumble, but every day, grace meets you where discipline cannot. Somewhere between rebuilding my body and rediscovering my own journey, I realized that my purpose couldn't expand if my well-being was contracting and my mission couldn't flourish if my body was failing. It was impossible to live up to my vision to transform others if it cost me myself. You can lead without well-being, but you cannot last.

The Premise: The Truth About Sustaining Your Life While You Lead

Well-being is the foundation of the Core 4. Even though it is the quiet center of every great leader's longevity, it is the part of leadership most often sacrificed, postponed, or negotiated away in the name of duty and ambition. It feeds the illusion that we can outrun our own humanity.

The modern leader isn't undone by a lack of talent or drive; they are undone by depletion. The destruction of well-being begins quietly with shortened patience, mental fog, irritability that slips into your tone before you've had time to hide it. At night, your mind refuses to power down, and in the morning your body feels like it's bargaining with you. These are signals from your internal world that your nervous system is overtaxed. You might have been trained to ignore them, but that can only delay the inevitable. Your nervous system is your first team. If it collapses, everything else falls.

The world praises resilience, agility, execution, innovation, endurance—but none of those muscles can fire when your internal battery is drained. Elite athletes understand this instinctively. They protect recovery with the same intensity that others chase achievement. They know that well-being is not what happens after performance; it is what makes performance possible. They treat restoration as readiness. They honor the truth most leaders avoid: You cannot outperform when you do not replenish what it takes to do so.

Well-being integrates the physical, the emotional, and the mental—the three systems that shape the quality of your presence and the longevity of your purpose. It is not a luxury, but an essential part of your strategy. You cannot neglect one without wounding the others. You cannot lead with clarity when your body is exhausted, your emotions are compressed, or your mind is overloaded. Your energy is not endless, but it is expandable. For Athleaders, well-being is not fragile, optional, or decorative, but foundational. It is the muscle that makes the rest of the Core 4 possible.

The Muscle: Well-Being

Well-being is the discipline of returning to wholeness—the daily practice of tending your mind, body, spirit, and energy so you can sustain your purpose with clarity, strength, and joy.

Well-being is the renewable power source of the Athleader—the internal ecosystem that fuels every decision you make, every room you stand in, and every pressure you carry. It is not a soft skill or a side practice; it is the physiological, emotional, and behavioral infrastructure that determines whether you can rise. Well-being is the culmination of how your body recovers, how your mind resets, and how your behavior protects what matters most. It is the muscle that modern leadership quietly depends on but rarely teaches you how to build.

At its core are **three performance capabilities**. Well-being is your capacity for sustainable energy performance—the ability to generate, regulate, and preserve the energy required to lead with clarity rather than exhaustion. Your physical readiness forms the foundation. When your body is depleted, your brain loses access to its highest functions: Decision-making narrows, emotional regulation weakens, creativity dims, and your stress threshold shrinks. Physical vitality isn't vanity; it is viability. It is the basic agreement you make with your future self: *I will not require more of my body than I am able to restore.*

But well-being is more than the body; it is the quiet repair of the inner world. Mental recovery and reset is the practice of uncluttering the mind so you can think with precision, even under pressure. Leaders often try to power through fatigue, believing that sharper thinking is a matter of effort rather than neurochemistry. Yet your brain cannot produce clarity when it is drowning in unprocessed stress, constant stimulation, and emotional overload. Mental reset is not an indulgence—it is neurological hygiene, the daily clearing of cognitive debris so your mind can operate at a strategic level rather than in survival mode.

And then there is the discipline that holds everything together: behavioral boundaries and focus, the choices that protect your energy from being scattered, siphoned, or silently stolen. Boundaries are not walls; they are agreements. They define where your attention goes and, therefore, what your life becomes. Focus is not a matter of willpower; it is the result of designing your behavior around what strengthens you instead of what drains you. When your boundaries are weak, everything becomes urgent. When your focus is fractured, everything feels heavier than it should.

When this muscle is neglected, leaders begin to unravel in ways they can't always name. The irritability that comes out sideways. They lose inspiration and struggle to recover from small setbacks. They feel a creeping resentment toward responsibilities that once felt like their calling. A leader running on fumes eventually becomes a leader running on fear, and that changes their mindset and their brain's physiology.

When the well-being muscle is strong, your entire operating system shifts. Your mind sharpens. Your emotional range expands. Your presence becomes more grounded and more generous. You begin to experience leadership not as a drain, but as a channel—one you can sustain because you are no longer leaking energy from every direction. You move through your days with steadiness. You recover faster. You make decisions from clarity, not fatigue. Pressure balances you instead of breaking you.

The Gap: Why Well-Being Breaks Down for Leaders

The modern world rewards exhaustion disguised as excellence. It praises the leader who pushes through, who carries more, who responds faster, who never lets the ball drop. But beneath that applause is a truth most leaders won't admit out loud: You can only sprint for so long before the sprint becomes your identity, and your nervous system begins to break under the weight of a pace it was never designed to maintain.

Burnout is the alarm that screams after years of ignoring the everyday erosion of well-being.

When physical readiness declines, leaders assume discipline will compensate for fatigue. But the body keeps its own score, and when your physical foundation weakens, your leadership becomes heavier, more reactive, and more fragile.

When leaders skip mental recovery, they convince themselves that they can think their way out of overload. But a cluttered mind cannot access creative insight, emotional range, or strategic clarity. Without a mental reset, you are thinking hard, but not well.

When behavioral boundaries blur, leaders gradually surrender their energy to other people's urgency. They say yes out of habit and accommodate others at the expense of their own stability, which destabilizes everything and everyone that counts on them. They allow their calendar to reflect everyone else's needs but their own. And over time, their life becomes crowded with obligations that drain them faster than they can refuel.

Too often, leaders believe that well-being will wait until later, after the deadline, or the quarter, or the busy season. But later never comes because the world is not slowing down. Leaders who wait eventually discover the most devastating truth of all: You cannot lead a life you are not well enough to carry.

When well-being is neglected, your gifts become harder to access. Your instincts dull. Your confidence shrinks. Your creativity narrows. Your relationships feel heavier. Your presence loses its warmth and becomes transactional. You start protecting yourself from the life you built instead of participating in it.

The Science: Why Well-Being Is the Engine of Sustainable Performance

Well-being may feel personal, intuitive, or even aspirational, but beneath every moment of stability, clarity, and sustained excellence sits a deeply biological truth: Your body and brain are performance systems. They respond to demand. They react to pressure. They register depletion long before you are willing to name it. And when leaders ignore those signals, they don't just lose energy—they lose access to the very functions that make leadership possible.

The research is unequivocal: Chronic stress without adequate recovery hijacks the prefrontal cortex—the center responsible for executive decision-making, emotional regulation, and strategic judgment.[41] When this region becomes overloaded, leaders experience what psychologists call cognitive thinning, a gradual narrowing of perspective, creativity, and insight. The brain shifts from visionary thinking to survival thinking. You start reacting rather than discerning, managing rather than leading.

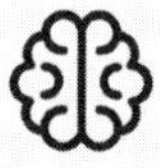 The nervous system becomes the first casualty in this erosion. Under sustained pressure, the amygdala becomes hyperactive, flooding the body with cortisol and adrenaline. This state was designed for short bursts of danger, not the prolonged demands of modern leadership. When the stress signal never turns off, your system loses its ability to return to baseline. Fatigue becomes your default. Irritability becomes a reflex.

Small obstacles feel larger than they are because your nervous system is already working at capacity. Well-being restores this baseline. Recovery isn't indulgence; it is neurological recalibration.

Physical readiness strengthens the body's capacity to generate and replenish energy, increasing blood flow, oxygenation, and metabolic stability. It's why elite athletes treat movement, hydration, and sleep as nonnegotiable. These are the biological conditions that allow performance to fire on command.

Mental recovery and reset reopen the pathways of clarity. When the brain enters restorative states, the hippocampus—the region tied to memory, learning, and emotional balance—repairs and reorganizes information. Insight returns, and your perspective widens. Emotions begin to steady.

Behavioral boundaries protect your nervous system from overtax. Every yes costs energy. Every demand on your attention reshapes your cognitive load. Boundaries preserve your ability to stay mentally present, emotionally available, and physically capable. They are a part of how you regulate yourself and your environment. Well-being expands your endurance, sharpens your clarity, and steadies your leadership under pressure. It is a biological requirement for sustained influence, longevity, and meaningful impact.

Athlete in Action:
Olympian Allyson Felix

There are moments in an athlete's life when the body whispers before it breaks, when the warning signs are quiet enough to dismiss but true enough to matter. Allyson Felix knows this terrain intimately. The world knew her as the most decorated US track athlete in history, a woman whose stride looked effortless and whose excellence seemed inevitable. But behind the medals and the speed was a truth she had never paused long enough to name: She had built her greatness on a body that she rarely allowed to rest. In 2018, that caught up with her.

Six months into a pregnancy she had long prayed for, Felix learned she had severe preeclampsia—a life-threatening condition silently unraveling her health from the inside out. One day, she was training, carrying both her child and her dreams. The next, she was rushed into an emergency C-section at 32 weeks, fighting for her own life and her daughter's. In her hospital room, she could no longer outrun what her body had been trying to tell her for years. Well-being is the foundation of performance.

Felix's comeback was not linear or glamorous. It began with learning how to walk without pain and breathe without fear. She needed to relearn how to trust her body after pushing it beyond its limits. The same body that carried her around a track at world-record speeds now required patience, boundaries, and grace. But alongside the physical rebuilding, a sharpening of conviction emerged. While she was fighting for her daughter's life, Nike was fighting to cut her contract. They offered her a 70 percent pay reduction because she was now a mother. Her pregnancy—and her near-death experience—was framed as a liability.

Felix returned to what mattered. She didn't just rebuild her body; she rebuilt the system around her. She walked away from Nike and testified before Congress about the maternal health crisis affecting Black women. She founded Saysh, her own shoe company, designed by and for women whose bodies are sources of strength. She returned to the Olympics and won more medals, this time wearing the shoes she designed. Her story is not about recovery. It is about well-being.

Felix teaches us that well-being is not the soft part of leadership, but the sovereign part. It is the moment you decide that your life, longevity, and legacy will not be sacrificed in the name of performance. It is the courage to say, "I will not lose myself to win for others."

When she stopped ignoring her body, her greatness expanded. Choosing motherhood multiplied her impact. As she allowed herself to heal and recalibrate, she confronted the costs of being strong for too long and she became a catalyst for change. Her story is the blueprint for the modern leader's well-being. Your health is not negotiable. Your body is not an afterthought. Your ability to flourish is the force that sustains your calling.

Athleader in Action:
Arianna Huffington

There is a part of Arianna Huffington's well-being story that most people never hear, because it took place long before the collapse that made headlines. It lived in the private spaces of her life—the late-night emails, the cross-continental flights, the quiet negotiations with exhaustion that she kept losing but refused to acknowledge. She had become the face of relentless achievement: bestselling author, media mogul, founder of the Huffington Post, a woman who moved with a velocity that made the world believe she was powered by something other than a human nervous system. But beneath the brilliance was a body whispering, then pleading, then finally demanding a truth she had spent years outrunning.

The moment she collapsed—striking the corner of her desk, waking up in a pool of blood with a broken cheekbone—felt sudden to everyone but her. What the world saw as an isolated event was, in reality, the inevitable consequence of a leader whose internal system had been compromised long before her body hit the floor. Her fall was not the crisis—it was the evidence.

In the months leading up to that moment, there were signs that her well-being was rapidly diminishing: memory lapses she brushed aside as busyness, emotional fragility she hid behind polished delivery, and a level of chronic sleep deprivation so normalized that she called it discipline. She had learned to perform strength long after her strength had been depleted. She had learned to endure what she should have questioned. And like so many leaders, she believed that well-being was something you earned *after* you succeeded—not what made sustained success possible.

She had built a life that could hold her ambition, but not her humanity. That realization arrived as a reckoning.

The rebuilding that followed wasn't about chasing energy hacks or productivity shortcuts. It was about confronting the deeper truth she had avoided—that exhaustion isn't a byproduct of leadership, it's evidence of misalignment. She began studying sleep, stress, burnout, and the physiological toll of performing at a pace the human body cannot sustain. She discovered the science she had ignored: that the nervous system is the foundation of performance; that chronic stress impairs memory, judgment, creativity; that the brain cannot sustain high-level thinking when the body is in chronic depletion. She learned that mastery without well-being is a house built on a cracked foundation.

And then she made a move most leaders fear: She changed the terms of her leadership. She stepped away from the company she built and founded Thrive Global—not as an escape hatch, but as an act of alignment and way to prevent other leaders from paying the price she had paid. Thrive was not born from burnout—it was born from clarity. Arianna finally understood the cost of the success that outpaced her well-being. Resilience without recovery is simply collapse delayed.

Today, Arianna's advocacy for sleep, micro-recovery moments, boundaries, and nervous-system conditioning is rooted in the wisdom of someone who learned that burnout is not a badge—it's a warning. Well-being is not a luxury, but the infrastructure for sustained impact. Her work is based on research; it's tested and strategic.

Arianna Huffington's story reminds us of a truth every Athleader must eventually face: You can build extraordinary things—but if you lose yourself in the building, the victory is incomplete.

The Reflection: Where Your Life Tells You the Truth

As we normalize fatigue, delay joy, swallow tension, and dismiss our aches as "just part of the job," our well-being and our body whispers truths we refuse to hear. There are long stretches where we function beautifully and feel terrible.

The same quiet pattern weaves through each of these stories: The body always breaks the silence first. Different stories reveal the same truth: Well-being is the first place misalignment emerges, and the last place leaders give themselves permission to pause. If you look closely, Felix, Arianna, and I reached a moment when willpower wasn't enough, when the next breakthrough required us not to push harder but to care more—for ourselves, for our bodies, for the lives entrusted to us. That is the moment well-being stops being optional and becomes essential.

Well-being is not a retreat from ambition. It is the steady return to the part of you that makes ambition possible. It is the discipline of listening before something collapses, restoring before something breaks, honoring your humanity before the world demands more of it.

Before you move into the drill, the practice, the rhythm, I want to offer you these questions:

Where is your life asking you to come home to yourself?

Where is your energy leaking?

Where is your joy thinning?

Where is your pace betraying your purpose?

❀ WELL-BEING PULSE CHECK-IN

1. What is draining me that I have been pretending is "fine"?
2. What part of my life needs margin, not more effort?
3. What is one reset—physical, emotional, mental, or spiritual— that I will honor this week?

The Conditioning:
The Reset Drill for Well-Being

A signature, system-wide drill for Athleadership. It helps restore executive function under pressure. It's designed to interrupt the hijacking of your mind when choosing the next step.

5 Words → 2 Boundaries → 1 Reset

Here's how it works:

Say (out loud or silently): **"Slow down. Come back home."**

These five words are your physiological reset—a direct signal to your nervous system to step out of overdrive and into regulation. They aren't meant to inspire you; they are meant to interrupt the silent escalation happening inside your body before your mind even notices the drift.

You may choose your own, or draw from these:

STEP ❶:

5 Words

- "My pace is my power."
- "Rest is strength, not pause."
- "I return to myself now."

When I whispered my own five words during that season of rebuilding—the season where my body was tired, my emotions were thin, and motherhood and mission were stretching me in opposite directions— something shifted. The tension eased. The noise softened. My body finally believed me when I said: "You don't have to be busy to be worthy." This is the beginning of well-being.

Boundaries are the power lines that protect your energy. Well-being isn't about indulgence; it's about protection. Set two honest boundaries:

- What is draining me right now? (Name the leak— physical, emotional, mental, relational.)

STEP ❷:

2 Boundaries

- What must I protect to stay well? (Your rest, your joy, your presence, your health, your family, your capacity.)

In my own season, the truth was sobering:

- *I was producing at a high level . . . and slowly abandoning myself.*
- *I was carrying everyone else's needs . . . and ignoring my own.*

Naming these two boundaries didn't solve everything, but it immediately restored clarity. When you tell the truth about what drains you and what protects you, the fog lifts. Your nervous system steadies. Your energy stops hemorrhaging. You return to your center.

Take one restorative action in the next 10 minutes. Forget the perfect wellness routine or life overhaul. Just choose one simple reset that signals to your body: "You matter, too."

Your reset might be

- A five-minute walk outside
- A glass of water before your next call
- Canceling a nonessential meeting
- Lying down for ten deep breaths
- Sitting in silence

STEP :

1 Reset

- Eating a real lunch
- Stepping away from a draining conversation
- Texting someone who brings you joy
- A weekend away

For me, during that season of rebuilding, the reset was simple but profound: Ask for help and make space—for healing, for coaching, for rest, for motherhood, for the woman I was becoming. That one reset became a rhythm. That rhythm became strength. That strength became my comeback. One restorative act rewrites the entire day. And well-being, practiced in small resets, rewrites your life.

The Everyday Example

Well-being is not only cultivated in mountaintop seasons or major life pivots. It lives in the overlooked moments where leaders abandon themselves in the name of responsibility.

Imagine you're a leader in back-to-back meetings, your screen is full, your patience thin, and your mind moving faster than your body can sustain. Your team thinks you're fine because you look fine—but internally, you're brittle, reactive, and running on fumes. Here's what well-being looks like in that sacred, everyday moment:

- You step out of the room—even for 60 seconds.
- You whisper your five words: "Slow down—come back home."
- Your breath returns.
- The tension releases.
- The overdrive finally softens enough for truth to surface.

Then the two boundaries arise:

- This pace is draining me.
- What I must protect right now is my presence and clarity.

From there, your one reset becomes clean:

- Close the laptop.
- Step outside.
- Drink water.
- Say no where you have been saying yes out of pressure.
- Reschedule what can wait.
- Protect what cannot.

One small reset restores your capacity, which step-by-step restores your well-being.

The Practice: Your Well-Being Activation

Here's how you embody well-being in real time using the Core 4 conditioning model tuned for your nervous system:

Pause + Return (*Drill*)

Say your five words slowly enough that your body believes them: "Slow down—come back home."

Name Two Boundaries (*Rep*)

- What is draining me right now?
- What must I protect to stay well?

Choose One Reset (*Rhythm*)

Pick one restorative action that returns you to center.

Rebuild Before Responding (*Recovery*)

Let your breath deepen. Let your body settle. Then return to the moment with clarity, not depletion.

This is not a checklist. This is how well-being becomes a lived practice—a daily act of sustaining your life, your leadership, and your legacy from the inside out.

The Integration: Where the Core 4 Becomes Your New Way of Leading

There comes a point in every act of becoming where the lessons stop living in separate rooms and begin speaking to one another. Where agility, resilience, alignment, and well-being are no longer ideas you admire, but instincts that rise inside you when pressure closes in. This is the moment where the Core 4 stops being a framework on a page and becomes the internal architecture of a leader who is built, not born.

It's easy to forget that leadership doesn't break down in the big crises—it breaks down in the quiet erosion of your internal system: the rushed mornings where you choose urgency over clarity, the long seasons where you survive change instead of steering it, the slow drift where your life looks full but you no longer feel connected to the person living it. This is where the Core 4 does its deepest work, not by helping you push harder, but by helping you return to yourself.

1. **Agility** teaches you how to meet pressure before it meets you, how to interrupt the panic, widen your choices, and move forward with clarity instead of fear.

2. **Resilience** restores your capacity to rise again, not by ignoring the bruises, but by learning how to turn disruption into direction.

3. **Alignment** brings your values, your voice, and your vision back into the same room, so your movement honors who you are becoming instead of who the world told you to be.

4. **Well-being** becomes the quiet power source beneath it all, the part of you that allows your greatness to be repeatable, not accidental.

And woven through each muscle is the system that makes them work: your mission, vision, and purpose (MVP), the compass that tells the Core 4 what to strengthen and why.

PART III

From Insight to Impact

Scaling Performance Through Culture and Practice

11

The 90-Day Way: Make It Repeatable

"Dreams are free. Goals have a cost. While you can daydream for free, goals don't come without a price. Time, Effort, Sacrifice, and Sweat. How will you pay for your goals?"

—Usain Bolt, Runner and Olympic gold medalist

There is a moment every leader knows too well: You wake up with clarity and go to bed wondering how you lost it. You start the morning with conviction—*Today I will lead differently*—and by mid-afternoon, that conviction has been swallowed by back-to-back meetings, relentless notifications, and a pace that bears no resemblance to the life you are trying to build. You didn't abandon your purpose. Your day simply never made room for it.

This is the leadership gap almost no one names. We believe we're leading with purpose, but our schedule is leading us. Regardless of our purpose, it cannot transform our life without behavioral patterns. What you need is a living rhythm, a way of moving through your days and weeks that keeps you

- **On Target**—anchored to your purpose (MVP)
- **On Task**—choosing the priorities that align with who you're becoming
- **On Time**—working in humane, sustainable 90-day cycles instead of endless pressure

Leaders don't burn out because their purpose is unclear. They burn out because their days don't match their purpose. You are about to make the shift from *knowing* your purpose to living from it on a Monday afternoon when the world is not cooperating. This is the moment when leadership becomes less about aspiration and more about architecture, how you actually move.

The 90-Day Way won't make you superhuman, but it will bring leadership back into a rhythm your humanity can trust—one quarter, one week, one day at a time.

It begins with a grounding question: If you were leading from your purpose tomorrow, what would a single day look like? Imagine a day driven by alignment, where your mental energy is focused instead of scattered, your boundaries support your well-being, your calendar reflects your Core 4, and your time mirrors your purpose instead of your inbox.

This is not about designing perfection. It is about revealing what matters most so that your *real* day can begin to reflect it. This vision—simple, honest, and human—becomes your direction, not your demand. It becomes the internal compass you'll return to as you build your quarterly rhythm.

The 90-Day Way is not a productivity hack. It is the structure that allows your MVP (mission, vision, and purpose), your Core 4, and your lived identity to finally work together instead of competing with the pace around you. This is how purpose moves off the page and into your daily decisions.

In practice, this distinction matters.

What ultimately distinguished leaders who sustained growth from those who regressed was not motivation—it was rhythm. These were leaders operating in complex, high-pressure environments, responsible for people, decisions, and outcomes that extended well beyond themselves.

They participated in structured leadership conditioning experiences designed to help them lead through sustained change and pressure, applying the work in real time as they navigated their roles.

Leaders who engaged in the work in the 90 Day Way were more likely to maintain behavioral gains and apply them consistently across changing conditions.

Over time, the data revealed something subtle but significant. Progress was not linear, but it was repeatable. Leaders who revisited their MVP, recalibrated the Core 4, and recommitted to practice showed greater steadiness in how they led others—not just themselves.

This rhythm did not eliminate pressure. It gave leaders a structure to move through it without losing themselves in the process. And when leaders practiced this rhythm together, the impact extended beyond individual performance into how teams operated and cultures formed.

This is where leadership stops being personal development—and becomes a system.

Why 90 Days Works

Every leader reaches a point where the pace of life outgrows the capacity of the body. We rarely name it. Instead, we push harder, stretch wider, and try to outrun the pressure with more effort. But the truth is simple and universal: Biology always wins. Your nervous system tells the truth long before your calendar does. According to Stanford's executive program, 90 percent of high-performing people do three things well:

1. Set specific goals with outcomes.
2. Set a deadline for their goals.
3. Write their goals down.

Most traditional goal cycles fall apart because one-year plans overwhelm our brains, and 30-day hacks cannot support meaningful change.

Ninety days is the rare and powerful sweet spot that is long enough to create real change and short enough to sustain commitment. It is the one cycle human beings can complete without collapsing under unrealistic expectations or losing clarity along the way. Neuroscience confirms we learn and hardwire new behaviors in 6–12-week cycles.[42] We are built for seasons—not sprints.

The 90-Day Way structures your life into four seasons across one calendar year, restoring the architecture you were designed for. Inside a 90-day window, something remarkable happens:

- **Your brain creates predictive loops.** The neural pathways that regulate emotion, stabilize decision-making, and keep you grounded when the environment becomes unpredictable.
- **Your habits move from effort to instinct.** Repetition begins to automate what once required willpower.
- **Your identity starts to shift.** Not dramatically, but steadily— the way a season changes, not a storm.

This is the same mechanism elite athletes rely on: build, refine, recover, repeat. Not a constant grind, but a functional cadence. A pattern your biology can trust.

The Three Pillars: How Change Becomes Lived

Most leaders try to change their lives through force: a surge of inspiration, a burst of willpower, a promise made at midnight after one too many exhausting days. But pressure has a way of revealing what we did not build. When the stakes rise, we don't rise to our goals; we fall to our patterns. If 90 days give you the architecture, these three pillars give you the engine—the living mechanics that turn intention into identity: reps, rhythm, and recovery.

Reps:
What You Repeat, You Become

Reps are the smallest unit of identity change. They are the quiet builders of confidence and capacity, actions so simple you almost overlook them, yet so consistent they rewire your brain's sense of who you are. Athletes use reps to create muscle memory; leaders use them to create mental muscle memory. A single rep rarely feels heroic:

- One centered breath before a difficult meeting
- One boundary honored instead of negotiated
- One moment of clarity before saying yes
- One step toward the outcome your MVP demands

But neuroscience is unambiguous: Repeated actions become automated, eventually integrating into our identity. And identity, not intensity, is what sustains leadership under pressure. Inside a 90-day cycle, reps protect you from emotional fatigue. They reduce cognitive load. They stabilize your focus so you no longer need to think your way through every challenge—your patterns do the work for you.

Rhythm:
The Cadence That Holds You When Pressure Rises

Rhythm is the internal pace you choose to lead from—the steady cadence that keeps you grounded even while your environment accelerates. When leaders lose rhythm, they lose coherence. They begin reacting instead of responding, sprinting instead of progressing, living in a pace that belongs more to expectation than intention.

Athletes never train at full intensity every day. Their seasons pulse: effort → integration → recovery → recalibration. This cadence preserves their longevity and protects their performance.

Leadership is no different. Your rhythm is what turns the 90-Day Way from hopeful planning into sustainable execution. It is how you

- Anchor alignment under pressure.
- Sense when agility requires a pivot.
- Practice resilience without self-punishment.
- Preserve well-being as infrastructure, not indulgence.

Rhythm says, "I can move fast without losing myself." This is how your nervous system learns to trust you.

Recovery:
Permission That Makes Performance Possible

In leadership, recovery is misunderstood and considered luxury, while athletes recognize it as an essential part of their strategy. Recovery makes your work sustainable by consolidating your thoughts, repairing your body, and regulating your emotions.

Most leaders don't burn out from effort—they burn out from the absence of recovery, which is an important distinction to understand. Recovery is the discipline of honoring your limits so your potential can expand. It allows your reps to take root and your rhythm to hold under pressure.

A New Pattern of Practice

Reps, rhythm, and recovery don't live in isolation. They come together to form a new pattern of practice for you. Your MVP sets your direction—who you are here to be and what truly matters. Your Core 4 tells you *what* needs to be strengthened in this season. Your 5-2-1 pattern of drills gives you the "how often" and "how deep." Together, they turn 90 days into more than a plan. They become your way of life.

Inside the Athleadership Arena, we build these with precision. So, how do you translate what you desire into a 90-day plan you can actually complete?

Building Your First 90-Day Way
(Step-by-Step, with MVP, Core 4, and 5-2-1 Woven In)

You don't need a perfect template to begin. All you need is a structure that is honest, human, and repeatable. The 90-Day Way is just that: a simple way to move from "I know my purpose" to "my days finally match my purpose." You've already done the hardest work—naming your MVP, facing your patterns under pressure, and strengthening your Core 4. This section is about translating that inner clarity into a 90-day rhythm you can actually live.

Think of what follows as a coach on the sideline, handing you a clear sequence.

Step 1: Start with One Core Intent (On Target)

Every 90-day cycle begins with a single clarifying question: *Over the next 90 days, what one core intent would create the highest lift in my life and leadership?*

Your Core Intent should sit directly on your MVP:

- **Mission**—the work you're here to do
- **Vision**—the future you're building toward
- **Purpose**—the why that makes it worth it

A Core Intent might sound like

- Lead with clarity instead of reactivity.
- Protect my energy so I can lead from overflow, not depletion.
- Align my role with the work that actually moves our mission forward.

If you're torn between options, choose the one that would make everything else easier or less frantic. Write it down. This is your north star for the next 90 days.

Step 2: Choose 2–3 Outcomes That Make It Real (On Task)

Once your Core Intent is set, translate it into a small handful of outcomes that are

- Specific enough to recognize
- Measurable in a real-life way
- Deeply tied to who you're becoming, not just what you're doing

Ask: *If I lived this Core Intent for 90 days, what would be different in my leadership, my work, my relationships, and my energy?*

You might name outcomes like

- My calendar reflects my top three priorities each week, not everyone else's urgency.
- High-pressure conversations end with clarity, not emotional residue I carry home.
- I finish most weeks with enough energy to be fully present with my family.

Now, **tag each outcome to one primary Core 4 pillar**, with a secondary if needed:

- Is this mostly about **agility** (adapting with intention)?
- **Resilience** (how you recover and rise)?
- **Alignment** (decision-making and integrity)?
- **Well-being** (how your system sustains the load)?

You're not filling out a matrix; you're giving your brain clear links:

This outcome is how I will practice resilience this quarter.

This outcome is how I will live alignment under pressure.

Now your plan isn't just a to-do list. It's targeted conditioning.

Step 3: Design Your Drills (The How)

Inside the Athleadership Arena, we go deep into the exact templates and tools. In this book, you simply need the pattern. Think of your conditioning cadence—a way to decide

- What you will repeat
- How often you will touch it
- When you will reset

At a high level, yours might look like

- Daily—A few short, daily reps that keep you aligned (micro actions tied to your outcomes/Core 4)
- Weekly—A practice to zoom you out (reflection, deep work, or journaling moments)
- A 90-Day Cycle—A deeper reset (a block of time to return, reset, and rewire)

You might not call them this in your calendar, but you live them as a pattern. To keep it simple, ask three questions:

1. **Daily:** *What are the tiny, repeatable actions that would keep my Core Intent in front of me?*
   Examples: one centering breath before each meeting; a two-minute alignment check before saying yes; a well-being boundary after a set hour.

2. **Weekly:** *When will I step back to see the week as a whole?*
   Examples: a 20–30 minute "film room" where you review what helped or hurt your Core 4; a brief planning block to align next week to your outcomes instead of your inbox.

3. **90-Day Cycle:** *Where will I put one protected window to look at the entire 90 days?*
   This is your deeper reset—the space where you practice return, reset, and rewire at the end of the cycle. You don't need to design an elaborate system. You just need to decide

   - These are the reps I'm willing to repeat.
   - These are the check-ins I won't negotiate.
   - This is the reset I will honor when the quarter ends.

That is more than enough to change your life.

Step 4: Put It on the Field

A plan that lives in your head will always lose to a calendar filled by someone else. You have

- 1 Core Intent
- 2–3 Core 4–linked outcomes
- A simple pattern of drills

Now, you take one more crucial step: You schedule what you say you value. You don't need to block eight hours. Start with

- A small daily window (even 5–10 minutes) for one or two key reps
- One weekly 20–30 minute check-in (your rhythm and reflection block)
- One date at the end of the 90 days labeled: Return/Reset/Rewire

This is where purpose stops being conceptual and starts becoming kinetic. The moment your plan touches your calendar, your future stops being abstract and starts making a claim on your present.

Expect Disruption and Plan to Adjust

The point of a 90-day rhythm is not perfection; it's *returning*. Life will interrupt. Urgency will surge. Some weeks, your 5-2-1 will wobble. That isn't evidence that the system failed. It's evidence that you're human—and that your system is finally honest enough to reveal where you drift. In the next section, you'll learn how to stay aligned when life doesn't follow your plan and how to return, reset, and rewire at the end of each cycle so your growth compounds instead of collapsing.

For now, remember this:

- Your **MVP** gives you *direction.*
- Your **Core 4** gives you *what to condition.*
- Your **5-2-1 drills** give you *the pattern.*
- Your **90-Day Way** gives you *the container* that makes it all livable.

You don't need to do everything. You just need to begin this quarter with one clear intent, a small set of outcomes, and a rhythm you're willing to practice.

A 90-Day Way Walkthrough (Example)

Imagine a leader named Jordan—steady, respected, relied upon by everyone but herself. Jordan wasn't struggling. She was simply stretched thin, operating at a pace that made purpose feel like a luxury and presence feel like a memory. When she reached this chapter, her MVP was clear on paper, but nowhere to be found in her day-to-day. It was

Mission: Build leaders, not dependency.

Vision: A team that performs without burning out.

Purpose: Lead from overflow, not exhaustion.

With that clarity in hand, Jordan moved into her first 90-Day Way.

1. **Her Core Intent (On Target):** She asked the question you just asked: *What is the one shift that would create the greatest lift in my leadership over the next 90 days?* Her answer surprised her with its simplicity:

   Core Intent: *Lead from grounded clarity instead of reactive urgency.*

This wasn't a goal. It was a recalibration—a return to who she wanted to be under pressure.

2. **Her 2–3 Outcomes (On Task):** Next, she translated her Core Intent into three outcomes tied directly to her Core 4:

   a. **Outcome #1 (Alignment):** *My calendar reflects my top three strategic priorities each week, not everyone else's urgency.*

   b. **Outcome #2 (Resilience):** *High-pressure meetings end with clarity, not emotional residue.*

   c. **Outcome #3 (Well-Being):** *I end most weeks with enough energy to be fully present with my family.*

She didn't chase everything. She named the few outcomes that would actually shift her life.

3. **Her Drill Patterns:** Jordan kept it simple:

Daily Reps

- A two-minute breath reset before every meeting (well-being).
- A single alignment question before each yes: Does this move my mission?
- A post-meeting note capturing one small win (resilience).

Weekly Practices

- **20-Minute Friday Weekly Reflection:** What helped? What hurt? What will I repeat?
- **Sunday Alignment Block:** 15 minutes to shape her week on purpose, not pressure.

One Cycle Reset (End of 90 Days)

- **A protected long weekend:** A time to reset (when she would focus on time to personally recharge).

You'll notice that Jordan is using drills differently from the Reset Drill in the Core 4. These tools are flexible, so use them however works best for you. The goal is to make this human and doable.

4. **What Actually Happened (Reality Meets Rhythm):** By week three, her plan cracked. Two team members resigned unexpectedly. A project shifted. Her 5–2–1 rhythm slipped. A month earlier, this would have triggered shame and over functioning. This time, she used her system:
   - She returned.
   - She recalibrated.
   - She reset the week with a smaller set of reps that were still aligned with her Core Intent.

This is where the real leadership was built: not in the flawless weeks, but in the way she recovered inside the messy ones.

5. **Her Results (Identity, Not Just Output):** By the end of the
    90 days,

    - Her team described her as *"calmer, clearer, and easier
      to follow."*
    - Her meetings were shorter because her alignment
      sharpened.
    - She ended each Friday with presence instead of depletion.
    - Her internal system—not her circumstances—set the tone.

Jordan didn't overhaul her life, but she built a rhythm she could live
inside.

This is the point of the 90-Day Way. It turns your purpose from a
statement into a structure—and that structure becomes a way of being.
The goal is not perfection. It is the intention to anticipate and pivot
through change and pressure. The key is consistency. Each time you
show up, you are building your leadership and your strength.

When Life Doesn't Follow Your Plan (Staying Aligned)

The moment you commit to a 90-day rhythm, something subtle
shifts around you. Not because the world has changed, but because your
intention has. Pressure begins to test the very structure you're trying to
build. A deadline compresses. A project expands. A family need arises
without notice. Someone on your team stumbles, and the weight quietly moves to your shoulders. The unexpected arrives—not to interrupt
your life, but to reveal your interior capacity.

This is the point where most leaders quietly fall out of formation.
Not because they lack discipline or desire, but because they were taught
to equate disruption with defeat. They assume that if the plan no longer
fits the moment, the moment has won. But leadership doesn't unfold in

perfect sequences. It unfolds in tension, in motion, in the gap between what you hoped would happen and what actually does.

Here is the truth that frees you: Every 90-day cycle fractures somewhere, not because you are inconsistent, but because you are human. Staying aligned is not about maintaining a flawless plan; it is about maintaining a faithful connection to yourself. Drift doesn't announce itself loudly. It appears in micro-signals: your tone shortens, your breath sits higher in your chest, your yeses multiply, your presence thins. You begin reacting to your environment instead of directing it. This is not failure. It is information.

And this is where your Core 4 stops being a concept and becomes a companion:

- **Agility** calls you back when you're clinging to how things "should have" gone. You feel the rigidity, the internal wrestling, the frustration that the plan isn't cooperating. Agility invites you to pivot without losing purpose.

- **Resilience** steps in when pressure compresses your confidence. Doubt rises. Energy dips. You question whether you're building or simply enduring. Resilience reminds you that recovery is not retreat; it is recalibration.

- **Alignment** reveals the drift before your results do. You start making choices that feel productive but not purposeful. Alignment pulls you back to your MVP—not as a slogan but as your internal compass.

- **Well-being** whispers what your mind tries to dismiss. Fatigue creeps in. Clarity muddies. You feel the emotional cost long before anyone else can see it. Well-being is the earliest indicator light on your internal dashboard.

These signals aren't indictments. They are invitations—quiet cues that your system is asking for attention, not punishment. This is the defining shift: Your internal scoreboard doesn't criticize you; it calibrates you. Your 90-day plan isn't a cage. It's an orientation system. When life moves—and it will—your work is not to abandon the plan but to adapt it with the same integrity you built it with.

Here, in this honest space of recalibration, the door opens to the next phase—the one that determines what you carry forward and what you release.

The Return, the Reset, and the Rewire

Every 90-day cycle ends the same way it began: with a moment of truth. Not a dramatic crescendo, not a performance review, but a quiet pause where you recognize that you are not the same person who crossed the starting line. Something inside you has shifted, subtly but meaningfully, and now you have a decision to make.

Many approaches skip this moment entirely, rushing you into the next demand without honoring what the previous season revealed. Athleadership does the opposite. Here, the end of a cycle isn't a finish line—it's a forge. The place where growth becomes wisdom and wisdom becomes identity. This closing triad—**return, reset, rewire**—is where transformation cements itself.

The Return: Coming Back Without Shame

Return is not about starting over. It is about coming home—to truth, to clarity, to yourself. Every leader drifts, breaks rhythm, and hits moments where the inner and outer worlds fall out of sync. Drift is friction that shows you where your next layer of growth lives. Return asks one thing of you: Tell the truth without punishment.

You review the cycle without distortion—where you rose, where you stretched, where you slipped. You acknowledge the choices that strengthened you and the ones that strained you. You give yourself credit for every place you stood strong and compassion for every place you could not yet.

The Reset: Clearing Noise, Reclaiming the Signal

Reset is where you release what no longer fits the leader you are becoming. Neuroscience calls this *cognitive unburdening*, interrupting old patterns so new ones can take root. You clear the emotional residue, the ineffective expectations, the overcommitments that diluted your energy.

Reset revolves around three questions:

1. **What needs to be released?**
2. **What needs to be recalibrated?**
3. **What needs to be recommitted?**

You let go of habits that drained you. You adjust rhythms that proved unrealistic. You recommit to the practices that restored you. Elite athletes never generate power without first releasing tension. Reset is that release.

The Rewire: Becoming the Leader Your Life Is Asking For

If returning brings truth and resetting brings clarity, rewiring brings transformation. This is where your brain consolidates the cycle into new pathways—through reflection, repetition, and embodied practice. Your responses shift. Your instincts sharpen. Your habits move from effort to instinct.

Rewiring happens because you stayed faithful to the work long enough for it to reshape you.

Where the Cycle Begins Again

Return. Reset. Rewire. This is not the end, but one part of a new pattern of living. Each cycle raises the foundation you stand on. Each return brings sharper truth. Each reset brings a cleaner focus. Each rewire builds a stronger identity. With each cycle, you rise. You become a leader who can meet whatever comes next because you've built a system inside yourself that does not break with the moment. And now, with this strength under your feet, you are ready for the final movement.

Crossing the Threshold

There comes a moment, after you complete your first 90-day cycle, when a quiet but unmistakable realization settles in your chest: You are no longer guessing your way forward. You are leading from a system you built.

Most leaders never experience this shift. They stay trapped in reaction, pacing their lives around whatever the world hands them. But you are not pacing anymore. You are choosing your work and directing your days with intention. You are becoming predictable to yourself, which is the foundation of trust, clarity, and power.

Once a leader builds a rhythm they can trust, they become a cultural force. Once a leader becomes aligned, resilient, agile, and grounded in well-being, they become the blueprint others silently follow.

This is where your personal transformation begins to ripple outward, and you shape the culture you lead.

12

Scale the System: Build the Culture, Become the Player-Coach

"Culture is what leads when no one is watching."

—Urban Meyer, 3× National College Football
Champion coach and author

There is a moment at the end of any true transformation when the world does not look different—but you do. It comes quietly, not with applause or the dramatic exhale you might expect from a moment of arrival, but in the subtle way your inner landscape has rearranged itself. After chapters of confronting illusion, reclaiming identity, meeting your pressure head-on, you arrive at a place you did not fully anticipate: a stillness that feels earned.

It happens in the soft space after you put in some work to make your 90-Day Way intentional—the moment you put down the pen or close the laptop and realize the plan you just built was never simply a plan. It was a mirror. It showed you the parts of yourself you'd hidden behind performance. It revealed the patterns that kept you sprinting without direction. It honored the resilience you cultivated in silence. And now, as you pause between the life you've lived and the one stretching toward you, you feel something rising—not adrenaline, not relief, but a deeper interior signal: You are no longer the person who began this book.

The realization arrives with gravity. Somewhere between naming the Performance Paradox, understanding your brain under pressure, strengthening your Core 4, and treating purpose as a practice instead of a concept, you crossed a threshold. You began leading yourself with the same intentionality you once reserved for leading others. You stopped moving from fear and expectation and began moving from alignment.

And now, in this final chapter, you understand what every elite athlete ultimately discovers: Mental personal mastery is only the first stage of greatness. There comes a moment when the growth that fortified you must ripple outward—into your team, your culture, your organization, your family, your future. This is not the moment where you "apply what you've learned" as an afterthought. This is the moment your transformation becomes inherited.

The real work of this book was to prepare you to become the kind of leader whose presence conditions the environment around them. You begin to see what the most impactful leaders eventually grasp— that inner evolution is not a private accomplishment; it is a responsibility. Your agility becomes a stabilizer that supports the people around you. Your resilience becomes an invitation for others to join you in a purpose-driven life. Your alignment becomes a pattern others can lean on. Your well-being becomes a standard that restores the humanity of the spaces you lead.

Athletic leadership was not born in theory; it was forged in the life of someone who once looked in the mirror, feeling broken, and still chose to rise. Neuroscience now validates that this is more than a metaphor; it is the conditioning that shapes how elite leaders rise, decide, and create winning impact. You have been building the internal architecture required to become a different kind of leader, one who not only survives pressure but transforms it. One whose identity is strong enough to serve as a blueprint. One whose presence becomes the arena where people rediscover their own courage, clarity, and capacity. The choices you make from here will one day become the model that carries someone else.

You are not at the end of a book. You are standing in a tunnel—the kind athletes walk through before the start of the game. Behind you is everything you've endured, practiced, and reclaimed. Ahead of you is the space where your private conditioning becomes a public force:

- This is the threshold where a leader becomes a player-coach.
- This is where personal mastery becomes cultural leadership.
- This is where your 90-day rhythm becomes a collective rhythm.
- This is where your identity becomes a catalyst.

And as the quiet truth settles deeper into your bones, you sense what every Athleader feels when purpose finally overtakes performance: You are ready—not because the world is easier but because you are stronger.

The Future Belongs to Player-Coaches

If the first part of your journey in this book asked you to reclaim yourself—to understand your identity, honor your nervous system, and rebuild the inner arena where purpose lives—this next movement asks something far more consequential: to redefine what leadership must become in a world that no longer slows down for anyone. Because the future will not belong to the leader who can simply outwork the moment, outtalk the room, or out-strategize the problem. It will belong to the rare leader who can do two things at once: Perform with excellence *and* elevate the excellence of everyone around them. The future belongs to the player-coach.

For too long, leadership models forced a false divide—either you were the one delivering results through sheer execution, or you were the one directing from above, separated from the friction of the work. But the speed and instability of the modern world have dissolved that divide. Today's organizations require leaders who can stay in the game without losing altitude to shape it—leaders whose identity is strong enough to hold pressure while their presence steadies the people they lead.

A player-coach is not the overextended hero who tries to do everything. A player-coach is a leader whose inner arena is conditioned enough to bring clarity into chaos, coherence into urgency, and stability into environments that once ran on strain. What they model becomes the real curriculum.

This is where the Core 4 becomes the defining infrastructure of modern influence:

- A player-coach moves with **agility**, not urgency, reading the field with clarity instead of reacting to noise.
- They model **resilience**, not bravado, recovering in real time in a way that teaches others how to rise without shame.
- They embody **alignment**, not performance theater, centering decisions in your mission, vision, and purpose (MVP), even when uncertainty intensifies.
- They steward **well-being**, not indulgence, proving that sustainable excellence is a strategic advantage, not a luxury.

When these dimensions are conditioned inside the leader's inner arena, leadership stops being a role and becomes a frequency. This is the real power of the player-coach: They don't manufacture culture—they transmit it. Their steadiness becomes a rhythm others can lean into. Their alignment becomes the quiet architecture of the team. Their resilience becomes a cultural permission slip. Their well-being becomes the guardrail that protects excellence from erosion.

This is the shift organizations struggle to articulate but unmistakably crave: Leaders who can generate performance in themselves and multiply it in others. Leaders who can coach without disappearing into oversight. Leaders who elevate standards without weaponizing them. Leaders who hold humanity and high performance in the same hand. This is why your journey matters.

Now you step into the role that defines the next era of your leadership: You become a multiplier.

The Inner Arena of Culture

Culture is one of the most misunderstood forces in organizational life—not because it is complex, but because leaders look for it in the wrong places. It does not live in values posters, dashboards, or mission statements. Culture lives inside people—inside the identities they carry, the stories they believe, and the nervous systems they bring into every room long before the first word is spoken.

Culture is the collective inner arena of a team. It is shaped by the emotional patterns that surface under pressure: what people fear, what they trust, how they respond when stakes rise, and whether they move toward each other or away. If leadership is personal, culture is patterned—and those patterns are either conditioned intentionally or shaped unconsciously by pressure.

Most organizations never look this deeply. They study performance metrics but not the emotional climate beneath them. They refine strategy while ignoring the internal rhythms of the people expected to execute it. They wonder why teams break down under stress, unaware that the system never strengthened the people who hold it up.

You've seen this before.

With an unconditioned team,

- A small setback spirals into blame.
- Meetings feel fast but fragmented.
- People wait for the "temperature" of the leader before they speak.
- Urgency becomes the atmosphere, not the moment.
- People hesitate to try new ideas because risk feels unsafe.

With a conditioned team,

- Pressure rises and clarity sharpens.
- Conflict becomes productive instead of personal.
- People speak honestly because alignment—not approval—guides the room.
- There is rhythm beneath the work, not adrenaline.
- People experiment freely because learning is safe.

Athleadership treats culture as psychology and physiology, not as branding. A culture is shaped by what leaders consistently embody, not by what organizations claim publicly. People learn leadership the way athletes learn excellence: by watching someone do it under pressure.

The best cultures—whether elite teams or high-performing companies—were not built by slogans or charismatic personalities. They were built by leaders solid enough internally to transmit stability externally. Culture is not what happens during the meeting; it is what happens after it ends. It is the emotional residue your presence leaves behind. It is the rhythm your team adopts because your identity taught them what steady feels like.

Your inner transformation did not stay inside you—it began to shape the environments you touch. This is the architecture of cultural change: Muscle Memory → Model → Mirror → Multiply. Condition the leader, and you condition the team and the culture, and high performance compounds.

The future belongs not to the organizations with the most strategies, but to those with the most conditioned leaders. Because leaders who are built from within create environments that outperform their circumstances—even when the world accelerates.

There comes a point in every organization's evolution when the problem is no longer strategy, capacity, or even talent—it's the absence of an internal system that helps people sustain who they are while delivering what the business demands. The pressure isn't the culprit; the pace isn't the villain. What breaks companies is the widening gap between the speed of change and the inner conditioning of the people expected to carry it. When that gap widens, culture frays, trust thins, and pressure begins to leak into every decision, conversation, and meeting until fatigue becomes the unofficial operating model.

I have watched high-performing teams crack not because they lacked intelligence or effort, but because their nervous systems were overwhelmed by the invisible tax of constant transition. I have also witnessed teams rebound—often quickly—when leaders anchored themselves, reset the rhythm, and re-centered the mission. You can feel the shift the moment it happens. Meetings become clearer. Tension dissolves. Decisions stop ricocheting. People find their footing again, not because the work changed, but because the *leaders did*.

This is the heart of the Enterprise Arena. Culture is not a brand aspiration; it is the collective inner arena of a team. It is shaped by how people breathe under pressure, how they recover after setbacks, how they navigate uncertainty, and how consistently they can return to alignment. Strategy may set the direction, but identity determines the execution. Culture is not built by artifacts or programs—it is built by the behavioral patterns leaders practice every day, especially when conditions tighten.

Some organizations still reward the visible—output, speed, results—because that is what they know how to measure. What they struggle to operationalize is the invisible architecture that generates sustainable performance: the agility that allows teams to adapt without fracturing; the resilience that keeps recovery possible; the alignment that reduces friction and clarifies priorities; and the well-being that protects long-term capacity. These four aren't "soft skills"; they are the performance infrastructure of modern enterprise, and when they are missing, organizations pay a cost far more expensive than training budgets. They pay what I call the transformation tax—the cumulative wear and tear that results when leaders navigate change without the internal tools to regulate, adapt, and respond.

I've seen this tax drain even the strongest companies. Productivity dips, but not evenly. Tension rises as people operate in survival mode. Collaboration erodes as urgency replaces clarity. High performers carry more weight until they burn out or disengage. The organization keeps accelerating its demands, hoping the next initiative or restructuring will solve what is, at its core, a *capacity problem*, not a commitment problem.

But the opposite is also true. When an organization learns how to condition its leaders from the inside out, the environment transforms. Decisions sharpen because leaders operate from alignment instead of panic. Collaboration strengthens because psychological safety becomes lived, not promised. Adaptation accelerates because teams know how to reset instead of spiral. Retention stabilizes because people feel built, not depleted. Innovation increases because resilience makes room for risk. All of this happens through a new *internal standard*.

Most companies want this; they simply haven't had a model to operationalize it. They know how to measure performance but not identity. They know how to teach skills but not conditioning. They can articulate their values, but they struggle to embed them in daily behavior under real-world pressure.

That gap is exactly why we built the Athleadership Arena for Business—not as a program to "teach leadership," but as a conditioning system that helps organizations build the inner arena their leaders were never taught to build alone. It provides a way to strengthen identity as intentionally as performance, to make culture conscious instead of accidental, and to scale the behaviors that turn mission and vision into lived reality.

How Your Team Moves Under Pressure

Every team carries a signature response when things tighten. I've watched teams who sprint into panic and teams who freeze into silence; I've seen rare teams who drop back into coherence because someone in the room holds their center. The pattern is never random. Pressure exposes whatever has not been practiced.

Ask yourself:

- When pressure rises, does this team return to its center—or scatter from it?
- Do decisions sharpen or blur?
- Do people anchor themselves or get swept into urgency?
- Does fear take the wheel, or does identity guide action?

How a team moves under pressure tells you everything about what has been conditioned—and what hasn't.

The Rhythm That Holds the Work Together

Burnout is almost never about workload alone. It is the consequence of a rhythm that never lets people return to neutral. Teams don't break because the work is hard; they break because the pace is ungoverned.

Ask:

- Are we operating from rhythm—or running on reaction?
- Do meetings begin grounded or already breathless?
- Do priorities shift with coherence or confusion?
- Is the team driven by noise or guided by intention?

Rhythm is not a luxury. It is the architecture that makes excellence sustainable.

The Identity Your Presence Conditions

Long before you give direction, your presence gives instruction. People read your nervous system—not your slide deck. They calibrate themselves to what you normalize.

Ask:

- What does my presence teach this team to believe is possible?
- Do they settle when you enter or tighten?
- Do they tell the truth because alignment is safe here?
- Do they learn recovery from watching you practice it—or exhaustion from watching you hide it?

Identity is always the real curriculum.

The Purpose That Aligns Every Level

Purpose is not messaging. It is a centering force—the stabilizer that keeps teams from fracturing under pressure. You've defined your MVP;

culture shifts when purpose becomes shared identity, not corporate language.

Ask:

- Do my people have a purpose they can name—and does it ladder into ours?
- Do individuals know why their work matters beyond output?
- Does the team understand the mission we share, the vision we're building, and the purpose that holds us when urgency rises?
- Is purpose alive in the room—or buried in a slide?

Purpose is alignment in motion.

Where It Starts

Transformation never begins with sweeping change. It begins with one shift in how you see your team, one adjustment in how you model identity, one practice that pulls people back to their center. If you want deeper diagnostic tools, the Athleadership Assessment offers expanded insight. But the most powerful transformation begins here—with your willingness to see your culture clearly and to shape it intentionally. Because leaders aren't born—they are built. And cultures are built by leaders who build themselves first.

The Leader's Legacy

There comes a moment in every leader's evolution when the pursuit of personal mastery gives way to a deeper, more consequential truth: Your growth was never meant to end with you. The work you have done in these pages—quiet, internal, often invisible—was not simply an act of self-restoration. It was a preparation. Because legacy, in its truest form, is not built in monumental gestures or end-of-career reflections;

it is forged in the daily, deliberate choices that shape how others experience themselves in your presence. Legacy is not what you leave behind when you are gone. It is what you build in people while you are here.

This is the quiet truth that separates those who lead teams from those who build cultures: People don't inherit your accomplishments—they inherit your conditioning. They absorb the way you pause before reacting, the steadiness in your voice when uncertainty rises, the discipline with which you protect clarity, the courage with which you return to your purpose when pressure tries to pull you away. Your presence becomes the template others calibrate themselves against, not because you asked them to, but because you showed them what becomes possible when a leader is built from within.

And now, as you stand on the other side of your own transformation, there is something essential you must know—something that marks this moment as more than a personal breakthrough. This is your new operating framework. This is your inner arena. This is the advantage most leaders spend decades searching for and rarely find.

Legacy is not an abstract ideal; it is a lived transmission. Every decision you make, every conversation you hold, every practice you repeat becomes a message about what leadership feels like in your care. Your children, your colleagues, your successors, and even the strangers who cross your path will inherit the emotional imprint of how you carried your purpose. They will remember whether your presence brought clarity or confusion, safety or strain, alignment or distortion. And it is here—right here—that your deepest responsibility emerges: to lead in a way that makes it easier for others to become who they were meant to be.

What you cultivate within becomes the world you create around you. What you normalize becomes what others believe is possible. What you practice becomes what others learn to repeat. This is how legacy moves—not in leaps, but in layers; not in declarations, but in demonstrations; not through authority, but through identity that has been strengthened and refined under pressure.

The Movement—The New League of Leaders

There is a point in every discipline where enough individual transformations begin to tilt the landscape—quietly at first, then unmistakably. Movements do not erupt from slogans or campaigns; they emerge from the steady rise of leaders who decide, often alone in the dark, to live by a different standard. Pause long enough, and you can feel it: You are standing inside such a moment now. The old playbook has thinned to the point of transparency, and a new kind of leader is being called forward.

Across industries, communities, boardrooms—even around kitchen tables—the world is aching for an archetype that no longer confuses exhaustion with excellence or constant urgency with real impact. People are searching for leaders who do not fracture under pressure, but convert it into clarity and contribution. Leaders who don't simply manage tasks but elevate people. Leaders whose presence steadies the room instead of tightening it. Leaders who are conditioned, not merely trained.

What you have been building within yourself—quietly, courageously, consistently—places you at the forefront of this new league of leaders. Not because you have perfected anything, but because you have chosen honesty over performance. Not because you escaped pressure, but because you learned how to meet it without abandoning yourself. You are becoming the kind of leader whose inner architecture is strong enough to shape the environment around them, the kind who carries the Core 4 as a lived frequency and the MVP not as a statement but as a source of light. The 90-Day Way is no longer a plan; it is the rhythm that guards your purpose inside chaos season by season.

Movements begin with leaders who dare to embody what others have only imagined. And what you are carrying now—your conditioning, your clarity, your reclaimed identity—is not simply personal growth; it is cultural potential. When one leader becomes grounded and aligned, the ripple is immediate: teams shift, meetings breathe, priorities settle, conversations deepen. I have watched the temperature of entire cultures change—not because of incentives, but because one person stopped being governed by survival and started being governed by purpose. If you step back, you can see the arc clearly now. You learned how pressure shapes the brain. You strengthened your Core 4. You defined your MVP. You built a rhythm through the 90-Day Way. None of these were separate tools. They were one system designed to help you lead from within when the moment asks more of you.

The Call-Up

This is the heart of Athleadership. Leadership becomes transformative the moment it becomes transmissible, and identity becomes culture the moment a leader embodies it consistently.

This is the legacy you carry forward. The field is open. The lights are up. The moment is asking for a different caliber of leader, one built from within, capable of performing when it counts and courageous enough to condition others through their own pressure. Everything you have learned now lives in you as a system you can return to in any environment, at any pace, under any pressure, at any season of your life. This is your call-up. Tomorrow, start small: Choose one conversation, one decision, or one meeting where you return to alignment before you respond. You've done the inner work. You know how to return to center. Now step onto the field—and become the leader the moment demands.

Acknowledgments

This work has been shaped by a remarkable community of leaders, thinkers, and believers who have stood alongside me in building what is now Athleadership.

To those who have endorsed this work—thank you. Your belief in this message and your willingness to stand behind it at this moment matter more than you know. I am deeply grateful.

To Michael Platt, PhD, thank you for lending your voice to this work through the foreword and for your pioneering contributions to neuroscience that powerfully affirm and elevate Athleadership.

To our Velvet Suite Board—Christine Cochrane, Francis A. Hondal, Elson Kuriakose, Letena Lindsay, Tanya E. Moore, and Julie Spencer Washington—thank you for your commitment to this vision and for the generosity of your wisdom, time, and passion. I am forever grateful.

To my mentors, Andy Steggles and Julie Wainwright—thank you for your wisdom, your belief, and your guidance. Your lived experience and insight is immeasurable.

To the A-Team at Velvet Suite—your belief, your excellence in execution, and your commitment to this work each and every day are what carry this vision forward.

To our inaugural Athleader Pros—Dr. Michael Mannino, Stephanie Johnson, LaChina Robinson, Tracey Newell, Charlie Batch, Ryall Graber, and Sagar Pandya—thank you for bringing your lived experience, your discipline, and your voice to this movement.

To our client companies and the extraordinary leaders I have had the privilege to work with—the executives, professional athletes, teams, and boardrooms I have been invited into—thank you for trusting me with your growth. You have shaped this work as much as I have.

To the global Athleader community—graduates across more than 26 countries who have been on this journey for two decades—thank you for learning, leading, and leaning into your mission, vision, and purpose. You are the legacy that will shape generations to come.

To those who have challenged me, stretched me, and held me accountable—thank you. You have made this work stronger. Your generosity, your belief, and the way you impact the world—both seen and unseen—continue to inspire me.

To my parents, my sister, family, my prayer circle, and my confidants—thank you for standing with me over the past two decades and lifting me up especially when I wanted to walk away.

Thank you to my publisher Ideapress who was a tremendous partner in bringing this book to your hands.

And to you, the reader—thank you for choosing to step into this work.

This book is not just something to read.

It is a lifestyle to be lived.

You've got this!

Glossary of Terms

Athleadership is the performance operating system for modern leadership—built on the elite athletic mindset and designed to condition the mental and neurological capacities leaders rely on to perform under pressure, adapt through accelerating change, and stay anchored to purpose. Grounded in neuroscience and proven in elite sport, it equips leaders to perform when it counts.

Athleader: A leader who is conditioned to perform under pressure, adapt in real time, and align their actions with a clear sense of mission, vision, and purpose. An Athleader doesn't rely on motivation or talent alone—they build the mental, emotional, and behavioral capacity to lead when it counts. Grounded in the Core 4 (Agility, Resilience, Alignment, and Well-Being), an Athleader consistently translates purpose into performance through disciplined practice, recovery, and execution.

Game: The game is the environment, the world—fast, unpredictable, constantly changing. It's everything that you cannot control. Leadership is played in two places: the game outside of you and the arena within you.

Arena: Your internal mindset. You can control it so pressure meets preparation, so who you are meets what's required. This is where you strengthen your leadership from within. Leadership is played in two places: the game outside of you and the arena within you.

MVP (Mission, Vision, and Purpose): This is your compass in chaos. This pillar defines who you are—because your identity becomes your compass. It clarifies what matters, sets your direction, and anchors your decisions so you can navigate challenges and pursue a version of success that is truly your own.

Mission: How will you accomplish the vision? (What will you do day in and day out?) The actions you take, the values you activate, the ways you serve each and every day.

Vision: Where do you aspire for your personal and professional life to go? (What is the destination?) The vivid picture of your future that pulls you forward, even when current circumstances don't.

Purpose: Why are you here? (What is the original intent and reason for being?) Why do you exist? Your unshakable reason for being—the deeper meaning behind your gifts, your grit, and even your journey. It is your power source and what uniquely defines your contribution.

The Core 4: Agility, Resilience, Alignment, and Well-Being. These four dimensions form the foundation of how you perform. Together, they act as your internal engine—stabilizing you under pressure, strengthening your capacity, and enabling you to rise to challenges with clarity and control.

Conditioning Practice: Performance is built through repetition. Conditioning is the intentional practice of training your mind, body, and nervous system to respond effectively under pressure. Through consistent reps, rhythm, and recovery, you build strength without depletion—rewiring how you think, act, and lead in real time.

The 90-Day Way: Sustainable change requires structure. The 90-Day Way is your execution rhythm—translating insight into action through focused, quarterly cycles. By operating season by season, you create clarity, maintain momentum, and build meaningful progress without overwhelm.

C > D: When the speed and complexity of change (C) is greater than the speed and depth of development (D).

The Performance Paradox: The gap between outward success and inward depletion. The Performance Paradox is the condition of being rewarded for the very behavioral patterns that erode your identity.

Identity theft: The identity slowly bargained away in exchange for belonging, approval, stability, and status.

Drills: Train your brain for the moment pressure hits by converting insight into instinct, awareness into action, and theory into muscle memory.

Reps: The smallest unit of identity change. They are the quiet builders of confidence and capacity, actions so simple you almost overlook them, yet so consistent they rewire your brain's sense of who you are.

Rhythm: The internal pace you choose to lead from—the steady cadence that keeps you grounded even while your environment accelerates. When leaders lose rhythm, they lose coherence.

Purpose-driven leaders: Those who put personal and professional meaning at the center of their work.

A player-coach: A leader whose inner arena is conditioned enough to bring clarity into chaos, coherence into urgency, and stability into environments that once ran on strain.

Transformation Tax: The cumulative wear and tear that results when leaders navigate change without the internal tools to regulate, adapt, and respond.

Your Next Move Starts Here

This is not the end of the work.

It is where it begins.

What you do next determines how you lead when it counts.

CONTINUE THE WORK

For organizations and institutions

Enter the Athleadership Arena: Build leaders who don't just understand performance but deliver it under pressure.

The Athleadership Arena equips your teams with a shared language, a proven conditioning system, and the structure to align, adapt, and perform in real time.

athleadershiparena.com

For keynotes, executive advisory, media, and partnerships

Bring Athleadership into your organization through high-impact keynotes and advisory designed to change how leaders think, decide, and perform under pressure.

melissadawnsimkins.com

STEP INTO THE ARENA

Leaders who sustain performance don't wait for the moment.
They condition for it. They are ready for it. Now it's your move.

Endnotes

1   McKinsey Global Institute, *The Social Economy: Unlocking Value and Productivity Through Social Technologies* (McKinsey Global Institute, 2012), https://www.mckinsey.com/industries/technology-media-and-telecommunications/our-insights/the-social-economy.

2   Emma Burleigh, "Brené Brown Warns American Workers Are Not Neurologically Wired for This Level of Rapid Change and Instability: 'People Are Not Okay,'" *Fortune*, October 21, 2025, https://fortune.com/2025/10/21/bestselling-author-brene-brown-workers-not-neurologically-wired-for-this-level-of-rapid-change-and-instability-geopolitics-ai-market-workers-mentally-struggling/.

3   Bryan Robinson, "Job Burnout At 66% In 2025, New Study Shows," *Forbes*, February 8, 2025, https://www.forbes.com/sites/bryanrobinson/2025/02/08/job-burnout-at-66-in-2025-new-study-shows/.

4   Elizabeth Woo et al., "Chronic Stress Weakens Connectivity in the Prefrontal Cortex: Architectural and Molecular Changes," *Chronic Stress* 5 (January 2021): 24705470211029254, https://doi.org/10.1177/24705470211029254.

5   Grant S. Shields et al., "The Effects of Acute Stress on Core Executive Functions: A Meta-Analysis and Comparison with Cortisol," *Neuroscience & Biobehavioral Reviews* 68 (September 2016): 651–68, https://doi.org/10.1016/j.neubiorev.2016.06.038.

6   Christina Maslach et al., "Job Burnout," *Annual Review of Psychology* 52, no. 1 (2001): 397–422, https://doi.org/10.1146/annurev.psych.52.1.397.

7   Stephan Dilchert et al., "Expanding Our Understanding of Quiet Quit-

ting: Antecedents, Correlates, and Consequences," *Human Resource Management*, December 10, 2025, https://doi.org/10.1002/hrm.70038. Popular discussions often frame quiet quitting as simple disengagement from work. However, research suggests it reflects a broader form of psychological withdrawal, extending beyond task disengagement to include reduced connection with colleagues and the organization, along with an increased emphasis on boundaries between work and personal life.

8   James E. Marcia, "Development and Validation of Ego-Identity Status," *Journal of Personality and Social Psychology* 3, no. 5 (1966): 551–58, https://doi.org/10.1037/h0023281.

9   Maslach et al., "Job Burnout."

10 Amy F. T. Arnsten, "Stress Signaling Pathways That Impair Prefrontal Cortex Structure and Function," *Nature Reviews Neuroscience* 10, no. 6 (2009): 410–22, https://doi.org/10.1038/nrn2648.

11 Robert M. Sapolsky, *Why Zebras Don't Get Ulcers*, 3rd ed. (Times Books, 2004).

12 Arnsten, "Stress Signaling Pathways That Impair Prefrontal Cortex Structure and Function."

13 Rajita Sinha, "Chronic Stress, Drug Use, and Vulnerability to Addiction," *Annals of the New York Academy of Sciences* 1141, no. 1 (2008): 105–30, https://doi.org/10.1196/annals.1441.030.

14 Gallup, *State of the Global Workplace 2025 Report*, 2025, https://www.equoranda.com/wp-content/uploads/2025/05/state-of-the-global-workplace-2025-download-1.pdf.

15 Bryan Kolb and Ian Q. Whishaw, "Brain Plasticity and Behavior," *Annual Review of Psychology* 49, no. 1 (1998): 43–64, https://doi.org/10.1146/annurev.psych.49.1.43.

16 Gallup, *State of the Global Workplace 2025 Report*.

17 Wolfram Schultz, "Dopamine Neurons and Their Role in Reward Mechanisms," *Current Opinion in Neurobiology* 7, no. 2 (1997): 191–97, https://doi.org/10.1016/S0959-4388(97)80007-4.

18 Bruce S. McEwen, "Physiology and Neurobiology of Stress and Adapta-

tion: Central Role of the Brain," *Physiological Reviews* 87, no. 3 (2007): 873–904, https://doi.org/10.1152/physrev.00041.2006.

19 Patricia Albulescu et al., "'Give Me a Break!' A Systematic Review and Meta-Analysis on the Efficacy of Micro-Breaks for Increasing Well-Being and Performance," *PloS One* 17, no. 8 (2022): e0272460, https://doi.org/10.1371/journal.pone.0272460.

20 Grant A. Pignatiello et al., "Decision Fatigue: A Conceptual Analysis," *Journal of Health Psychology* 25, no. 1 (2020): 123–35, https://doi.org/10.1177/1359105318763510.

21 Nick Craig and Scott A. Snook, "From Purpose to Impact," *Harvard Business Review* 92, May 2014, https://hbr.org/2014/05/from-purpose-to-impact.

22 Aliya Alimujiang et al., "Association Between Life Purpose and Mortality Among US Adults Older Than 50 Years," *JAMA Network Open* 2, no. 5 (2019): e194270, https://doi.org/10.1001/jamanetworkopen.2019.4270.

23 Pignatiello et al., "Decision Fatigue."

24 Deloitte, *2021 Deloitte Global Human Capital Trends: The Social Enterprise in a World Disrupted* (Global, 2021), https://www.deloitte.com/us/en/insights/topics/talent/human-capital-trends/2021/social-enterprise-survive-to-thrive.html.

25 Bogdan Draganski et al., "Changes in Grey Matter Induced by Training," *Nature* 427, no. 6972 (2004): 311–12, https://doi.org/10.1038/427311a.

26 Eran Dayan and Leonardo G. Cohen, "Neuroplasticity Subserving Motor Skill Learning," *Neuron* 72, no. 3 (2011): 443–54, https://doi.org/10.1016/j.neuron.2011.10.008.

27 EY Global, "Why a Female Athlete Should Be Your Next Leader," 2020, https://www.ey.com/en_au/athlete-programs/why-a-female-athlete-should-be-your-next-leader.

28 Eleanor Frankel, "Sports & Leadership: Lessons Learned in Sports Have Helped Johnson Graduates Succeed in the Business World," *Cornell SC Johnson College of Business*, 2019, https://business.cornell.edu/hub/2019/01/11/sports-leadership/.

29 Alimujiang et al., "Association Between Life Purpose and Mortality Among US Adults Older Than 50 Years."

30 Vladyslav V. Vyazovskiy and Kenneth D. Harris, "Sleep and the Single Neuron: The Role of Global Slow Oscillations in Individual Cell Rest," *Nature Reviews Neuroscience* 14, no. 6 (2013): 443–51, https://doi.org/10.1038/nrn3494.

31 Alimujiang et al., "Association Between Life Purpose and Mortality Among US Adults Older Than 50 Years."

32 McEwen, "Physiology and Neurobiology of Stress and Adaptation."

33 Bryan Kolb and Robbin Gibb, "Brain Plasticity and Behaviour in the Developing Brain," *Journal of the Canadian Academy of Child and Adolescent Psychiatry* 20, no. 4 (2011): 265–76.

34 Clough, Peter, and Doug Strycharczyk. *Developing Mental Toughness: Improving Performance, Wellbeing and Positive Behaviour in Others.* London: Kogan Page, 2012.

35 Arnsten, "Stress Signaling Pathways That Impair Prefrontal Cortex Structure and Function."

36 Joseph LeDoux, "Rethinking the Emotional Brain," *Neuron* 73, no. 4 (2012): 653–76, https://doi.org/10.1016/j.neuron.2012.02.004.

37 Arnsten, "Stress Signaling Pathways That Impair Prefrontal Cortex Structure and Function."

38 George Bush et al., "Cognitive and Emotional Influences in Anterior Cingulate Cortex," *Trends in Cognitive Sciences* 4, no. 6 (2000): 215–22, https://doi.org/10.1016/S1364-6613(00)01483-2.

39 Arnaud D'Argembeau, "On the Role of the Ventromedial Prefrontal Cortex in Self-Processing: The Valuation Hypothesis," *Frontiers in Human Neuroscience* 7 (2013): 372, https://doi.org/10.3389/fnhum.2013.00372.

40 Eddie Harmon-Jones, ed., *Cognitive Dissonance: Reexamining a Pivotal Theory in Psychology*, 2nd ed. (American Psychological Association, 2019), https://doi.org/10.1037/0000135-000.

41 Harmon-Jones, *Cognitive Dissonance*.

42 Phillippa Lally et al., "How Are Habits Formed: Modelling Habit Formation in the Real World," *European Journal of Social Psychology* 40, no. 6 (2010): 998–1009, https://doi.org/10.1002/ejsp.674.